# LETTERS
## TO
# THE EDITOR
### that were never published
#### (and some other stuff)

## ALEX CAEMMERER JR. M.D.

Order this book online at **www.trafford.com**
or email orders@trafford.com

Most Trafford titles are also available at major online book retailers.

Printed in the United States of America.

ISBN: 978-1-4669-0337-1 (sc)
ISBN: 978-1-4669-0336-4 (hc)
ISBN: 978-1-4669-0335-7 (e)

Library of Congress Control Number: 2011919837

*Trafford rev. 11/08/2011*

 www.trafford.com

North America & International
toll-free: 1 888 232 4444 (USA & Canada)
phone: 250 383 6864 ♦ fax: 812 355 4082

# Contents

# Introduction

THE NEW YORK TIMES IS like no other newspaper on Earth. Decision-makers here and around the globe read it with very special interest, both for its intelligent reporting and in hopes of seeing their own doings validated in the opinions expressed on its pages.

It is an encyclopedic chronicle of local, national and international events in business, the arts, show biz, sports, food, society, science, religion, history, military affairs, medicine—in a word, a universal compendium of contemporary knowledge and developments from around the world. Its scope and seriousness make it an extraordinary resource that offers the regular reader a lifetime of learning.

Perhaps most interesting of all is the editorial section, comprising in-house editorials, usually on topics of the day, and the op-ed page, which is devoted to major contributions by outstanding authorities in various fields. There is also a section set aside for Letters to the Editor from readers wishing to express an opinion on a recent article. The chances of one's letter being published are slim, on the order of one in a thousand—that being the number of letters received each day!

I have become addicted to writing letters to the Editor of The New York Times, and have been fortunate enough to see a handful of my letters make it into print. At the same time, over the last decade or so I've written well over a hundred letters that were not published, so I decided to take advantage of the opportunities which now exist to get them into print by other means.

Here, then, are my letters to the editors of the New York Times, The Record (an excellent newspaper published in Bergen County, N.J.), Newsweek, Business Week, the New York Post and Psychiatric News, a specialized publication for psychiatrists, of which I am one. I have also included a small collection of essays on topics of interest to me which I hope will also be of interest to my readers.

Many of the letters are on the same or related subjects; I have tried to keep overlap to a minimum without compromising the coherence of each.

# Credits

I AM INDEBTED TO MY SON John Caemmerer for editing the text and to my son Alex Caemmerer III for coaching me through the intricacies of preparing this book for publication on the computer.

I would also like to express my sincere gratitude to Scott Grey, Bernard Gaines and Nick Arden of Trafford Publishing for their expert and friendly assistance.

# Dedication

TO MY WIFE LI AND my sons John, Alex III and William, for giving me a happy life.

# Chapter 1

# PSYCHIATRY

THE HISTORY OF PSYCHIATRY DATES back to the Middle Ages, when the mentally ill in Europe were placed in the 'oubliette,' a hole under the street covered by an iron grate over which the rest of the citizenry casually strode while going about their daily activities. Later, here in America, elderly women suffering from senile psychoses, delusions, hallucinations, etc. who happened to live in Salem, Massachusetts, were charged with witchcraft and executed, usually by hanging. Not much changed in the United States until the Civil War, when Dorothy Dix changed things forever with her campaign for decent care for the mentally ill. Hospitals arrived on the scene, and at least some attempts were made to care for the seriously mentally ill in a humane way, though at that time there were no effective treatments available.

Earlier, in the 1840s in France, Franz Mesmer had demonstrated a hypnosis-like procedure that could be used to calm hysterical patients. It was even used as anesthesia in surgical procedures. Then Pierre Janet, the French psychologist, introduced hypnosis and demonstrated that hysterical symptoms, frequent in mid-19th-century France, responded to this procedure.

Then along came Sigmund Freud, who took an interest in Pierre Janet's work on hypnosis. He went on to be the first to describe a psychological theory of mental functioning and introduce psychoanalysis, the first systematic psychological treatment of what were then called neuroses. During the 1930s a large number of psychoanalysts emigrated to America where they started a major movement and established institutes for the training of psychiatrists in psychoanalysis. Psychoanalysis dominated the scene for outpatient therapy throughout its heyday in the 1940s, 50s and 60s. During that period a number of analytic institutes were established in the United States and there evolved a number of different 'psychoanalytically oriented' psychotherapies, including some very innovative approaches to the treatment of psychological disorders.

The 1950s saw the arrival of the first really effective antipsychotic and antidepressant medications. They were so effective, in fact, that they changed just about everything in the field. Previously, the severely ill had been housed in massive state hospitals where the only treatments available were electroconvulsive (shock) and insulin coma therapy. The early antipsychotic medications suddenly made it possible for patients to be discharged, and some of the state hospitals were closed. The follow-up for most patients, however, was woefully inadequate, with the result that many severely ill people are now in jails, where they are isolated and mistreated, often abused, and certainly don't receive the medical treatment they need. The rest of this chapter goes into more detail on this subject and traces the development of present-day methods for the treatment of mental illness, including their advantages and disadvantages, mistakes which have been made, and their limitations due to financial and other causes.

\*     \*     \*

## TO THE EDITOR OF THE NEW YORK TIMES:

Much has been written about the disastrous and inexcusable deinstitutionalization of the mentally ill during the past several decades. The increased need for community-based facilities for these patients was not met by the mental health system, which in turn led to an escalation of the process and deadly consequences. Most of these patients suffer from what we now know to be highly treatable diseases of the brain. Paradoxically, the new medications which are so effective in relieving symptoms and allowing people to live productive lives are just what enabled the mental hospital system to discharge them en masse. This amounted, however, to an abandonment of many patients to the streets. Only minimal facilities were provided for follow-up treatment, let alone any kind of housing arrangements. A frequent corollary of severe mental illness is that those suffering from it also lack insight into their condition and are therefore unable to seek out or cooperate with treatment.

Many of those discharged from state hospitals landed in New York City penniless and of those, many sought shelter in the Port Authority Terminal or on Central Park benches, having nowhere else to sleep. This became such a distressing situation to mental health professionals, that a group of psychiatrists got together and volunteered to track down these patients to evaluate them, see to it they had medication and urge them and help them to seek shelter in the facilities available in the city.

Society continues to view the mentally ill with contempt, preferring to ignore their plight until a healthy member of society is assaulted by someone who is mentally ill. Only then is society motivated to do something—not to help the mentally ill, but to isolate them to protect the rest of us.

The recent shameful headline in the New York Post demanding that the "crazies" be gotten off the streets epitomizes our society's hostile and compassionless attitude toward a very sick and mistreated group of our fellow citizens. If our political leaders are so interested in saving money, why don't they dump all the children in foster homes onto the streets? It is accurate to say that these children would be better able to fend for themselves than many severely mentally ill adults. Most people would feel sorry for the children and actively demand that something be done to help them. In the case of children, there would be a quick and effective response to such a breach of civilized behavior, and yet mentally ill adults are comparable in their neediness.

# TO THE EDITOR OF THE NEW YORK TIMES: OCTOBER 22, 2003

## Dorothy Dix, Where Are You Now?

The present shocking and shameful way in which we treat the 'mentally ill'—the common pejorative term for patients suffering from diseases of the brain—is actually the logical consequence of specific actions and attitudes. The care of psychiatric patients in New York State, and in much of the nation, is now again what it was in the middle of the 19th century when Dorothy Dix started her revolution.

The well-meaning but badly planned and grossly inadequate follow-up after the ill-fated deinstitutionalization of psychiatric patients several decades ago allowed government agencies previously responsible for such care to drop the ball, unchallenged, in order to save money. The medical insurance industry, taking its cue from these events, used to deny adequate coverage for psychiatric disorders in order to save money, under the mistaken assumption that funding treatment on a parity with other illnesses would cause costs and premiums to soar. That it has been able to get away with this is no doubt due to the persistent stigma attached to mental illness and the perception that it is not a legitimate medical condition.

One branch of psychiatry, namely psychoanalysis, has not helped in this regard. The rise in the 20th century of psychoanalytic theory and practice to an elitist and self-appointed status of dominance has tended to distance the treatment of psychological disorders from mainstream medical practice. All mental disorders, even obviously organic brain diseases such as schizophrenia, were viewed as purely 'psychological' or the result of 'severe psychological regression.' Only recently has the psychoanalytic community finally come around to recognize the biological and biochemical causes of the major mental disorders.

Even Freud said that merely studying the psychological manifestations of mental disorders and that the major breakthroughs would one day be made in the study of brain biology. This day did come recently, but neither the analysts nor the insurance companies wanted to accept it.

The brain is an organ and, like the other organs (liver, pancreas, thyroid, etc.), it has its own physiology and biochemistry. All mental functioning is accompanied by chemical and physiological activity in the neurons. The psychological cannot be separated from the biological, that is, from physiology and chemistry. One of the foremost neurobiologists of our time described psychotherapy as the neuronal activity of a therapist acting on the neuronal activity of a patient.

A few states have enacted so-called parity laws requiring medical insurance companies to cover treatment of 'biologically based' mental illnesses. Unfortunately, this has turned out to be a vague concept and is easily circumvented to avoid coverage. The trauma of 9/11, for instance, caused many psychological reactions resulting in biologically based disorders, and these can be effectively treated by a combination of psychotherapy and medication. Is post-traumatic stress disorder psychological or biologically based? The answer is that it responds to the judicious use of both modalities.

The newer psychotropic medications, the selective serotonin reuptake inhibitors (SSRIs) and their cousins, have proven effective in treating many psychiatric disorders, much to the surprise and gratification of everyone, especially the patients. Although these substances are referred to as antidepressants, they would be better described as brain-normalizers, because that's what they seem to do and that is how patients themselves describe the effect they have. The new antipsychotic medications have also changed the lives of many of the thousands of patients suffering from major brain disorders.

The cost of both hospital and outpatient treatment is high. As the article points out, however, $200 million are right now being spent on building new jails in New York State, where many severely ill psychiatric patients have unfortunately landed and where they are subjected to isolation and cruelty but receive no medical treatment. Meanwhile, does anyone, including the insurers, object to cardiac bypasses costing $100,000 each or cancer chemotherapy, which at

$10,000 a shot not infrequently ends up costing well over $100,000 for a year's treatment? Did anyone bat an eyelash at the $1,000,000 for the recently publicized surgery to separate conjoined twins from Central America? For some patients, MRIs and CAT scans costing $1500-$2500 each are routinely ordered several times a year and paid for without question.

Diseases of the brain should be brought into the mainstream of medical care and accorded the same level of interest and concern, treatment, insurance coverage and respectability by the entire medical community as any other disease. From a cost standpoint it has been shown, in fact, that when psychiatric services are readily available, other medical services are used less.

Let's bring the manner in which our society deals with the enormous burden of psychiatric disorders into the 21st century and quit denying the fact that it is a major problem and cannot be addressed effectively using our present approach. No money is being saved—quite the opposite—by persisting with what has been failing for decades.

## TO THE EDITOR OF THE RECORD:

The recent apparent suicide of a patient out on pass from the psychiatric division of the Bergen Pines County Hospital in Paramus, New Jersey, has resulted in criticism of its professional staff and calls for the dismissal of administrative staff as well. This is not where the blame belongs.

Sweeping changes in the funding and delivery of medical care in general, and mental health care in particular, have put all providers under pressure to emphasize time and cost over quality of care, with the result that doctors are no longer able to give patients their best.

Pressures from government, insurance companies and HMOs force hospitals to discharge patients as early as possible, without regard to their condition or degree of recovery—witness the policy in some states of discharging new mothers the day after delivery!

The situation is particularly acute when it comes to the criteria for admission and discharge of psychiatric patients. In the past, any person with a serious psychiatric illness could be admitted to a hospital involuntarily without the requirement that they be considered dangerous, and discharge was conditional only on the staff's assessment that the illness had stabilized.

The new requirement that a patient represent "a danger to self or others" focuses only on one point in the complex course of an individual's illness and inherently increases the risk of undesirable outcomes in the handling of a case. In discharging patients, mistakes in clinical judgment using the *illness* criteria can usually be corrected by prompt follow-up treatment in an outpatient facility. Errors in predicting *dangerousness* are not simple to correct, however, and have too often resulted in tragic consequences.

The critical problem is that predicting dangerousness is much more difficult than diagnosing serious psychiatric illness, since it is more easily covered up and therefore more difficult to assess. Its presence often eludes detection even by skilled practitioners. Years ago, an American Psychological Association task force on violence concluded that psychiatrists could not be expected to accurately predict violent or suicidal behavior in patients. In fact, the study indicated that family members were better able to predict suicide than psychiatrists. Our society, however, apparently expects psychiatrists to do it with 100 % accuracy!

The result is that too many patients are being discharged from psychiatric facilities before their condition has stabilized, since this is no longer the criterion for discharge, as it should be. Until this policy is changed, the number of tragic outcomes will continue to grow. In the meantime, don't blame the psychiatrists and hospital administrators. Blame the budget-cutting politicians and insurance carriers who hold the purse strings.

It is conceivable that this issue might one day pit insurance companies against each other. After all, the money that medical insurers are saving thanks to the practice of prematurely discharging seriously ill patients from hospitals will have to be paid out—and then some—by malpractice insurers in the form of hefty awards to the families of those patients when they commit suicide, as a predictable number of them will.

I am sure that psychiatrists would gladly go back to using purely medical criteria in admitting and discharging patients from hospitals. The ACLU would object, no doubt, but then again they're not the ones who are responsible for patient care. Certainly the patients and their families would be better served.

## TO THE EDITOR OF PSYCHIATRIC TIMES:

## How Times Have Changed!

Reading your recent article "Treatment Success Hinges on Unique Alliance of Psychiatrists, Patients," I was struck by how much the practice of psychiatry has changed over the last half-century. There was once a time when we had virtually no effective psychotropic medications, whereas now we have such effective ones that most psychiatrists actually confine their practice to supervising their use, leaving the role of the psychotherapist to non-medical mental health professionals.

I began my training in the field with residencies at the NYS Psychiatric Institute and Bellevue Psychiatric Hospital in the late 1940s, when hospitals were full and treatment of psychiatric disorders consisted mostly of electroconvulsive therapy (ECT), insulin coma therapy, psychosurgery and a few other somatic treatments. Private practice consisted in either psychoanalysis or else any of a number of gradually evolving psychotherapies, ranging from what was known as 'psychoanalytically oriented psychotherapy' to interactional, transactional, client-centered, behavior modification, hypnotherapy, etc. The only medications available were barbiturates for sedating disturbed inpatients, although ECT was also used for immediate control of very disturbed patients.

Psychoanalysis, of course, was entering its heyday at that time. But since the analytic institutes had limited space, many of those entering the field of psychiatry actually received their supervision in psychotherapy from analysts. Soon a literature developed in the various modifications of analysis and psychotherapy. This made treatment more available, especially to those who couldn't afford the time and cost of the years of daily sessions which a commitment to analysis required.

Then, in the mid 1950s, along came the antipsychotics and the antidepressants. The former allowed the mass discharges of patients who had hitherto been warehoused in the state hospitals, and the latter offered a more acceptable and available treatment option for both inpatients and outpatients with depression. However, these medications had their disadvantages: the severity of their side effects precluded their use in many patients, they led to many cases of suicide and overdoses were lethal.

In those days, psychiatric residency programs emphasized the teaching of psychotherapy in outpatient departments, often supervised by psychoanalysts, but increasingly by psychotherapists as the latter became more numerous and experienced and as the literature developed.

Then along came Prozac, the first of the SSRIs and their cousins, which are not only more effective for most conditions, but have a more rapid onset, cause fewer side effects and are virtually never lethal, unlike the first generation of antidepressants. In addition, these medications are what I call brain normalizers, since they are not only uppers, but are also effective for both depression and anxiety, as well as many other disorders. I have seen these medications virtually turn patients' lives around, with therapeutic effects evident after only a few weeks instead of many years of classical analysis. (I am reminded of two attendees at a recent drug-company-sponsored meeting on medications who described themselves as "former psychoanalysts.")

As these medications have come into widespread use, and somewhat influenced by HMO cost-cutting efforts, psychiatrists have begun to specialize more and more in psychopharmacology, leaving the psychotherapy to non-medical therapists such as social workers and psychologists, who are less expensive for the HMOs.

By limiting their practice to brief medication-monitoring visits, psychiatrists can also significantly increase their income, since in most cases a 15-minute monitoring visit is reimbursed at half the rate of a 45-minute psychotherapy session.

One consequence of this is that the teaching of psychotherapy has largely disappeared from residency programs. Patients are now being seen by non-medical psychotherapists, who may refer them for evaluation, prescription and medication monitoring by a psychiatrist in what is called combined treatment. However, studies have shown that this treatment option is neither as cost-effective nor as therapeutically effective as when the psychiatrist does both.

The thesis that the therapeutic alliance is important in psychiatric treatment is such a basic concept that the fact that the article has to even bring it up, much less defend it, I find appalling. How did we get to this point, anyway? Did anyone ever really think that all it would take would be to write out a prescription? Is there no recognition anymore of the powerful effect of the therapeutic alliance—the listening, relating, understanding, acceptance, support and respect of the therapist for the patient? Has the whole concept of a doctor-patient relationship been forgotten in this scientific and technological day and age? I read recently that medical schools are now instituting courses on how to listen to patients—once the sine-qua-non of psychiatric practice. It used to be the accepted universal and essential qualification for the psychiatrist, and gave rise to the famous joke with the punch line "Who listens?"

In my own practice, after evaluating a patient I never prescribe medication until the second visit at the earliest, for if I do there is no way of knowing whether the patient's mental state on the second visit is the effect of the initial interview or that of the medication. Quite often on the second visit patients say they feel much better even when no medication was prescribed. If medication is initiated immediately, how can its effectiveness be evaluated?

I also feel sorry for those psychiatrists who haven't had training in psychotherapy. To me it is the most interesting part of practice and the most rewarding; offering insights to patients that result in behavioral changes and the eventual discontinuation of medications gives me a feeling of accomplishment. Don't get me wrong; these newer medications are marvelous, but they're not the whole answer. Good psychotherapy, supported by medications to relieve disabling symptoms, can be very effective in helping patients mature psychologically, modify their self-perceptions, and relate more realistically to the people in their lives.

## TO THE EDITOR OF THE NEW YORK TIMES:

### The Sad Case of Dr. Levin

The article "Talk Doesn't Pay, So Psychiatry Turns Instead to Drug Therapy" (Sunday, March 6, 2011, p. A1) describes the sad story of Dr. Levin, a psychiatrist who only does the pharmacotherapy part of what is known as 'combined therapy,' in which the psychotherapy part is handled by a non-medical therapist. Studies have shown that combined therapy is more expensive for insurance companies than when a psychiatrist does both, as the latter is more effective and quicker. I myself am a psychiatrist of Dr. Levin's generation, and I do both, enjoy my work immensely and am more effective and experienced than ever. The thought of retirement fills me with dread; I would be bored to death—literally! My patients appreciate me; they say "Where were you 20 years ago when I needed you?" I hear something new every day, something that I have never heard before—it's like an endlessly interesting story unfolding before my eyes. One fast rule I have is that I never give medications on the first visit, because on the second visit I often hear patients say "I feel better already." (The new medications are miracle drugs—I use them generously and you can turn people's lives around with them. But it's only with psychotherapeutic discovery, in other words conversation, that I can facilitate maturity and deal with identity problems, which are what patients often bring as their chief complaint these days. I would guess that Dr. Levin would agree with me, since he says "All of my patients leave me unfulfilled. I miss the mystery and intrigue of psychotherapy. Now I feel like a good Volkswagen mechanic." He says he does what he does so he and his wife can retire comfortably. (You'll be bored to death, Doctor.) His wife says, "Medication is important, but it's the relationship that gets people better." (Well said!) He says, "People want to tell me about what's going on in their lives, and I am forced to keep saying 'I'm not your therapist.'" The fact that patients say they want him to be their therapist means that they develop immediate positive transference to him, an indication of a good therapist and necessary for good therapy. He admits that the quality of the treatment he offers now is poorer than what he did when he was younger. (How sad!) He expresses some surprise that his patients admire him as much as they do. (This, to me, suggests he has an identity problem.) He says, "The sad thing is that I'm very important to them, but I barely know them." I would tell him, "Dr. Levin, what a shame that you are depriving your patients of your experience and talent!" (Given a chance, I think I could help this man really enjoy the rest of his life!) Dr. and Mrs. Levin are trapped in their fear of an unaffordable retirement.

## TO THE EDITOR OF THE NEW YORK TIMES:

## Psychological Services on College Campuses

In the very enlightening and encouraging article in the Education Life Section, one commenter suggests that the increasing use of psychological services on college campuses might be a sign that therapy has lost its stigma, at least among college students. It has, in fact; and this has occurred in the general population as well, due probably to the increased emphasis in the profession on the biological causes of mental illness and the use of psychotropic medications in treatment to supplement psychotherapy. Many mental health professionals decry this increasing emphasis on and use of medication, but it is just this emphasis that has lessened the stigma of mental illness. If one speaks of 'brain diseases' and offers treatment with what I call 'brain normalizers'—the newer SSRIs and their cousins—the idea of being treated for a mental problem becomes acceptable to more patients. It gets them in the door, and treatment modality can then be decided. Patients understandably find it easier to accept the idea of having a 'chemical imbalance' than they do being labeled a 'psycho.' It is still true that in many people's minds psychiatric diagnoses and theories of causality sound pejorative and suggest weakness of character. This is what stigmatizes. Studies have shown that men, in particular, consider it a sign of weakness to consult a psychiatrist for depression, with the result that the depression goes unrecognized and untreated, often with very unfortunate outcomes. In fact, these conditions are now highly treatable and sometimes respond quite spectacularly.

## TO THE EDITOR OF THE RECORD:

## Psychological Effects of the 9/11 Disaster

Society has traditionally tried to label people with psychiatric conditions as being different from so-called normal people by using such pejorative terms as 'crazies,' 'nuts,' 'psychos,' etc., to refer to anyone seeing a 'shrink.' The latter term, also pejorative, serves to cast the psychiatrist as a fool and thereby deny him or her the credibility to diagnose mental illness. Such is the fear in our society of being seen and stigmatized as 'crazy.'

The recent September 11 disaster, meanwhile, has given rise to a great variety of symptoms of anxiety and depression in many otherwise normal people, if not the whole nation: disturbed sleep, nightmares, panic attacks, persistent images of the actual attack and its aftermath, fears of returning to work in the city, avoidance of places reminiscent of the attack, fears of crossing the George Washington Bridge, reduced interest in entertainment in public places such as theater, eating out and concerts, and, of course, sadness. Anxiety and depression can also manifest overtly or else as a whole range of physical symptoms. The anthrax scare, with its implication of the possibility of a broader bioterrorist attack, increased everyone's fears another notch. Such stressors can accumulate and cause or intensify pathological reactions in anyone, whether or not they have a psychiatric disorder to start with.

What becomes evident in these widespread symptomatic reactions to extreme stresses is that almost everyone, to one degree or another, is vulnerable to traumatic events and can develop psychological symptoms. Those most severely affected may require crisis intervention to avoid further deterioration of their condition. Others may seek out help voluntarily to find some relief.

To deal with people in distress from the recent traumatic events, the American Psychological Association set up emergency consultation services at Pier 94 in New York City staffed by volunteer psychiatrists, psychologists and social workers—'mental health providers,' as we are known these days. Demand for these services has been high, and they have been effective and greatly appreciated. It's worth noting that the services in question have been advertised as 'counseling' rather than 'psychotherapy,' 'psychiatric consultation,' or 'crisis intervention,' which are the terms traditionally used for mental health services of this kind. Most likely it was felt that there would be less stigma if the 'psych' part was eliminated in favor of the more friendly term 'counseling'—a fact which itself is an indication of attitudes towards all things psychiatric.

Perhaps people will one day come to understand that the difference between the average 'normal' person and someone receiving psychotherapy is only a matter of degree; anyone can be exposed to stressors, and when a person is in enough pain, he or she rises above the stigma and seeks help. People with psychological disorders are not a different breed of human being.

Many people with a mental illness are never diagnosed or treated, and the result for them and their families is a lot of suffering, disability and disordered lives. This might change as a result of the disturbing events in the weeks following September 11.

As my grandmother used to say, "It's an ill wind that doesn't blow somebody some good."

[Note: On August 7, 2011, the Times reported on a sizable number people who had experienced severe traumatic effects from the 9/11 attack and who, despite ongoing treatment, were still experiencing disabling symptoms a decade later.]

# TO THE EDITOR OF PSYCHIATRIC NEWS:

## "We Don't Get No Respect"

Rodney Dangerfield's famous line rings true for us psychiatrists. What we do has been suspect for a long time. No one hesitates to use the pejorative term shrink or other put-downs, and you often hear psychotherapy referred to in the media disparagingly as 'talk therapy.' Surgery, for some reason, is rarely belittled as 'knife therapy' or the 'carving treatment,' nor do you often hear internists as a group dismissed as 'medicine men.' In my dealings as a psychiatrist with some of the managed care companies, I have heard care managers justify their requirement that the need for the care I provide be recertified every 6 or 8 sessions by saying "We don't want our members to spend their time just chatting about their daily doings." Upon hearing that I am seeing a patient once a week, they suggest "What about seeing this patient every other week?" as if half the number of sessions would be just as effective—after all, it's only talk therapy. Even one reviewer—a psychiatrist—once said to me, "I know your patient needs treatment, but I have to worry about the bean counters."

Care managers appear to think psychiatrists keep their patients in treatment frivolously just to keep their hours filled. They clearly have no confidence that we can be taken just as seriously, and are providing treatment which is just as essential, as 'real' medical specialists. I once asked a care manager if she would ever deny a patient an MRI, to which she replied "Of course not!" I have had care managers—most of whom are social workers, nurses or psychologists—make suggestions as to how I should handle my patients. One, without even knowing a particular patient's condition or mental status, suggested his treatment be reduced to monthly medication monitoring. (For the record, prescribing a change in treatment amounts to practicing medicine, and doing so without having examined the patient amounts to malpractice.) I have had suggestions that I switch a patient to group therapy made to me by people who have no understanding of the indications for that form of treatment.

That psychiatrists can and often do turn people's lives around doesn't seem to figure in the perception of our role in medicine that is held by care managers—or the public in general, for that matter. People generally just seem to assume that we psychiatrists are either incompetent, ineffective, dishonest, unethical, hard up for patients or that we enjoy sitting in our offices chatting with patients for our own amusement because we have nothing else to do. That we might actually be working, with therapeutic goals in mind, for the benefit of people in distress who need our help doesn't seem to be part of people's picture of what we do. Certainly psychotherapy is not seen as a serious contribution to a patient's welfare or curative of anything—for that you need medications! (In fact, medications are extremely effective—and especially so, as reliable clinical studies have repeatedly shown, when used in conjunction with psychotherapy.)

When I inform insurance company care managers that I get numerous requests for appointments every day and have no difficulty keeping my practice full, they are surprised. The honest ones confide to me that they, too, realize that their job is primarily to save money for the insurance company, that the company is not interested in seeing patients get the treatment which is most effective and that the system is biased in the company's favor. The rationale given is that we psychiatrists have to be monitored lest we give unnecessary treatment, that is, drag the treatment on arbitrarily or for our own gain, and the presumption is that it isn't really of much real medical value at all anyway. They say "I'll give you 8 sessions" as if they are doing me and the patient a favor, rather than admitting that their purpose is to dole out sessions, and therefore patients' benefits, as sparingly as possible. (Not all insurance companies are guilty of this. Some are genuinely interested in seeing patients get the amount of treatment they need, even by psychiatrists.)

The only solution to this unfortunate situation is the proposal now being considered by Congress, namely, complete parity for psychiatry with other specialties. It really should happen and I predict it will happen. Only then will our profession, unlike Rodney Dangerfield, get the respect it deserves. I further predict that if psychiatric treatment is made more accessible there will be proportionately less utilization of other medical specialties— and then we will see truly substantial savings.

## TO THE EDITOR OF THE NEW YORK TIMES:

### On Parity for Mental Health Coverage

In your reporting on the controversy over parity in insurance coverage for mental health treatment, the main concern seems to be "to prevent the unnecessary use of mental health services." There seems to be a perception that people consult mental health professionals frivolously and that therapists enjoy dispensing 'non-treatment' to people with no psychiatric disorder. This perception couldn't be further from the truth. (Why is it that no one is concerned that people will go to orthopedic doctors and talk them into applying casts to unbroken legs?)

In fact, most people with a psychiatric illness stay away from psychiatrists and other mental health workers too long because of the stigma society places on both the illness and the treatment. I have been a practicing psychiatrist for many years. My observation is that people frequently endure severe and painful conditions for years, if not decades, before seeking treatment. Men in particular try to solve their depressions—the most underdiagnosed and undertreated condition in medicine—with alcohol and promiscuity. Not only is this ineffective, it actually makes the eventual treatment more difficult and prolonged, and therefore more costly. And as for the idea of treating non-existent conditions, I wouldn't know how or where to begin, since I have had no experience or training in 'treating' healthy people. What would I prescribe for someone with no symptoms? How would I know what medication would be effective in treating nothing? Meanwhile, there is no dearth of those in genuine need—I have to turn patients away almost daily. In any case, I would think it would be quite boring; treating real conditions is much more satisfying and rewarding.

Let me go further and say that, in fact, I have saved insurance companies untold thousands of dollars by taking over the treatment of hypochondriacal patients who might otherwise have spent the rest of their lives needlessly and endlessly incurring specialty consultations, MRIs, CAT scans and other expensive diagnostic procedures—all ordered to reassure both doctor and patient. By trying to limit access to mental health treatment insurance companies are going after nickel-and-dime stuff. If they really want to save money, they need to go after the big stuff.

## TO THE EDITOR OF THE NEW YORK TIMES:

## The Parity Bill Fails in the House

The Times (November 6 and December 19, 2001) reported that under the pressure of "furious lobbying" by HMOs, the House failed to pass the mental parity bill already passed by the Senate. This is a good example of the short-sightedness of insurance companies, who claim to be interested in saving money.

In the first place, the goal of "preventing unnecessary treatment" suggests that mental health workers treat healthy people. This is totally erroneous. (Do orthopedic doctors put casts on unbroken bones?) In fact, the opposite is true. Large numbers of people needing psychological care have such an aversion to seeking it that many go on suffering for years instead of getting the help they need.

In the second place, "containing mental health costs" is going after nickel-and-dime stuff. If insurers really wanted to cut costs, they would go after the big-ticket items— expensive diagnostic procedures like MRIs, CAT scans, echocardiograms, etc. Often these procedures are ordered merely to reassure anxious patients (and their doctors). The cost of one MRI or CAT scan would pay for 6 months of psychotherapy. One coronary bypass would finance a year of psychiatric treatment for half a dozen patients. A couple of bypasses would pay the yearly salary of a full-time psychiatrist. From my own experience, the medical testing lavished on patients with anxiety states, panic attacks and other psychological disorders would pay for the psychotherapeutic treatment they really need many times over—for years, if necessary (which it usually isn't).

Many studies have shown that access to mental health care reduces the use of other medical resources. Insurance companies could save some real money if they just did a little homework!

[Note: After a long struggle, the U.S. Senate (in 2007) and the House of Representatives (in 2008) finally passed a parity bill into federal law.]

# TO THE EDITOR OF NEWSWEEK:

## A Shrink Talks Back

After reading Sharon Begley's "Get Shrunk at Your Own Risk" (Newsweek, June 18, 2007, p. 49), I couldn't wait to write this letter. In the first place, the title is grossly inappropriate and demeaning to mental health professionals. Calling us headshrinkers, even in jest, is unacceptable and only plays into the lingering stigma associated with psychological treatment. I doubt that the author, if she had been writing about ineffective or botched surgery, which also does occur, unfortunately, would have chose the title "Get Butchered at Your Own Risk." As for her views on antipsychotic medications, she should have been around before they existed, as I was, when all we psychiatrists could offer schizophrenic patients was electroconvulsive (shock) therapy, insulin coma therapy and trans-orbital and frontal lobotomy, none of which even came close to offering the benefits modern medications do (never mind the side effects!). The newer antidepressants also have side effects, but believe me, they can and do frequently turn people's lives around. To my mind, they are miracle drugs. I call them *brain normalizers*. Ms. Begley is no doubt right that there are some inexperienced psychotherapists experimenting with untested approaches who should be better monitored, but that is no reason to question the value of the wide range of highly effective psychotherapeutic and pharmacological treatments that are available now. As for the author's comments on dissociative identity disorder, that is an area that has had little attention and one which presents problems that not many therapists have experience handling. Some therapists may decide to try innovative methods in an attempt to reach these patients, who are very difficult to work with. In fact, such patients may only be able to get help from inventive, pioneering therapists who are willing to stick their necks out and explore newer and less proven techniques. The assertion that 10-20% of all patients who receive psychotherapy are harmed by it sounds way out of line. If I found that this was happening in my practice, I would quit tomorrow! (It sounds more like the percentage of patients who are not helped, rather than the percentage harmed.)

# TO THE EDITOR OF NEWSWEEK:

## It's Our Turn

Psychiatry has been the stepchild of medicine for too long. It's high time we were accepted by mainstream medicine as legitimate specialists and accorded the position of importance we deserve. Instead, we are regularly referred to using such pejorative terms as shrinks (short for headshrinkers), nut-doctors and psycho-doctors. As Rodney Dangerfield says, we don't get no respect. Another interesting phenomenon: when a primary care physician refers a patient to a psychiatrist, the patient feels rejected and even insulted. Being diagnosed with a psychiatric disorder feels to some people like being told they have a weak character. Similarly, when a patient chooses to see a psychiatrist, the primary care physician is the one to feel slighted. Everyone finds something to feel bad about when a person needs to see a psychiatrist. Rounding out the picture is the odd fact that people outside the profession act like they know all about psychiatric illnesses and can speak with authority on the subject—the only medical specialty of which this can be said.

When I started out as a resident physician in the late 1940s the only treatments available for psychiatric patients were psychoanalysis for outpatients and hospitalization for those with severe conditions. Hospital treatment was mostly custodial care for patients whose behavior was deemed unacceptable or dangerous to society and consisted of either electroconvulsive therapy (ECT) or insulin coma treatment. Psychosurgery was also coming into use, though results in difficult cases were quite modest. ECT was and still is the most effective and safest treatment for severe depression, but its use declined for two reasons: it became politically incorrect after movies like *One Flew Over the Cuckoo's Nest,* and the first effective antidepressants came along. Though quite effective, this first generation of antidepressants had unpleasant side effects that often precluded their use. They were also lethal and unless closely monitored could result in death by overdose.

Psychoanalysis became popular when large numbers of European analysts, most of whom at that time were Jews, emigrated to the United States to escape Nazi persecution. However, analysis was time-consuming and very expensive and therefore not within the reach of most psychiatric patients. (Nor, incidentally, was it ever clinically proven to be safe or really effective for any condition. Its popularity was mostly due to its novelty and anecdotal reports of cures.) As a result, out of necessity and general interest a variety of what were called dynamic or psychoanalytically oriented psychotherapies were created. As the scientific literature around them grew, so did training opportunities, and before long these therapies became accessible to more patients and, together with medications as they became available, became the mainstream form of psychiatric treatment.

With the second generation of antidepressants, the most noteworthy of which are the SSRIs (selective serotonin reuptake inhibitors), we now have medications which are very effective, clinically proven and mostly very safe. Their use in conjunction with dynamic insight therapy and cognitive therapy now makes it possible to treat a variety of psychiatric disorders quite effectively. Freud himself, in fact, predicted this development. He said that he was only studying human psychology and that the most important advances in psychiatric treatment would come from the study of brain physiology and biochemistry. This is exactly what has happened, and some of the treatments we use now rival anything that psychoanalysis ever hoped to accomplish and produce those results in much less time. With a combination of medications and judicious psychotherapy, we can now turn people's lives around.

Unfortunately, despite these enormous strides the field of psychiatry continues to be viewed with skepticism and held in low regard, both by other physicians and the public. People are reluctant to acknowledge our accomplishments dispassionately and without prejudice and accept us as major contributors in the treatment of many conditions.

Two recent items in the press demonstrate my point. One concerned the dismay that orthopedists are experiencing at the ineffectiveness of their surgical treatments for back pain. The headline of a recent article in the New York Times quoted an orthopedic surgeon as saying "26 billion is spent on back surgery each year and we don't know whether it helps." They also acknowledge that "in 85% of cases, we don't know why the patient feels back pain." Well, in psychiatry we have known for a long time that in about 85% of cases the pain is psychosomatic, that is, it is due to spasms caused by emotional stress, etc. These cases can be treated successfully with psychotherapy, either alone or supplemented by an anxiolytic (anxiety-reducing) medication. The second article reported that women suffering from depression are at greater risk than other women for heart attacks. In the past, cardiologists would scoff at such a notion—just as they once scoffed at the idea that diet and exercise were important in the causation and treatment of cardiac conditions.

Depression is just about ubiquitous in our society these days, costing billions of dollars in lost working time, and yet it is the most underdiagnosed and undertreated of all medical conditions. Primary physicians often don't recognize depression in their patients or are reluctant to refer them to psychiatrists. Even if they do, patients are then often reluctant to follow through on the recommendation. As a result, only a small fraction of depressed patients ever gets adequate treatment, and it's partially because these illnesses are not considered important, psychiatrists are not respected for their ability to treat patients and the public still fears the stigma and disgrace of being labeled a 'psycho.' Medical doctors, who generally dismiss psychosomatic conditions as unworthy of serious attention, are still telling patients "It's all in your head" without offering them any treatment options. Male patients with depression then attempt to treat themselves with alcohol and extramarital sex, neither of which solve the problem.

Another phenomenon which has accompanied the advent of very effective medications is that many psychiatrists now confine themselves to medication monitoring, leaving the psychotherapy part to non-medical psychotherapists—social workers and psychologists. Many of the latter are skilled professionals, but it has been shown that treatment is more effective when both modalities are done by the psychiatrist. Unfortunately, HMOs have encouraged this splitting of roles, which is called 'combined treatment,' because the non-medical therapists cost them much less. Some psychiatrists actually prefer this arrangement, since they can make more money by doing the shorter medication supervision sessions than they can doing psychotherapy. In my view, they are missing out on the most satisfying part of the job—and the most effective form of treatment.

Rather than seeing psychiatrists as 'shrinks' who have little to offer and are to be avoided at all costs, people should realize that we are often in a better position to offer a non-judgmental setting where people can talk about their most private thoughts and feelings than are priests, ministers, close friends or relatives. An experienced psychotherapist can effect profound changes in people's lives, their relationships, their work and, most importantly, in their own perception of themselves—what is commonly known as self-esteem and identity. Psychotherapy touches people's lives more intimately than any other branch of medicine. And rather than being stigmatized or seen as having a character weakness or dependency issues, those who seek out psychotherapy should be seen as saying yes to possibilities for psychological growth, increased maturity, personal security and self-awareness of a sort that many people never experience. Psychiatrists should be respected for their major contribution to the prevention and treatment of 'dis-ease' in many, many patients. Our medical colleagues should welcome our contributions and insights, not view them with skepticism and distrust.

## TO THE EDITOR OF THE NEW YORK TIMES:

## On Alzheimer's Disease

The front page article in today's New York Times on elderly people's fears of developing Alzheimer's Disease or other dementias includes mention of the phenomena commonly known as the 'senile moment.' Although frequently viewed as an ominous early sign of dementia, it is in fact not a memory defect but rather a perfectly normal slowing of retrieval experienced by most people as they get older. The woman who describes her technique of going through the alphabet to summon up a name she is having trouble remembering is using an effective method to facilitate retrieval. It's also a good exercise for improving memory function, even in old age. It's comparable to doing a search on a computer, in that you set a process in motion which, even if it's not immediately successful, continues while you turn you attention to other matters, and then the answer 'pops up' later.

## TO THE EDITOR OF THE NEW YORK TIMES: JANUARY 9, 2011

## The Tragedy in Tucson, Arizona

Although at this time the mental status of the perpetrator in the shootings in Tucson, Arizona, is not known, there is a strong possibility that he was suffering from a severe mental illness. This situation is reminiscent of the shootings last year of 31 people at Virginia State University by a man who had been known to have a severe psychosis. Some time ago in the field of mental health the rules and criteria for admission and discharge of psychiatric patients were changed. In the past, any patient with a serious psychiatric illness, dangerous or not, could be admitted to a hospital involuntarily and would be discharged based only on whether the illness had stabilized and not merely based on a judgment that the patient was no longer dangerous.

The consequences of an error in clinical judgment of *dangerousness* are far more serious than those of an error made in assessing *illness*. Unfortunately, instances of misjudgments of dangerousness are all too common and often result in tragic consequences, including both suicidal and homicidal outcomes. Predicting dangerousness is much more difficult than diagnosing a serious psychiatric illness. Dangerousness in a patient often goes undetected even by skilled mental health professionals. In fact, years ago an American Psychiatric Association task force on violence concluded that psychiatrists could not be expected to accurately predict violent or suicidal behavior in patients. Thus, too many patients are being discharged from psychiatric facilities before their condition is stabilized, since this is no longer the criterion for discharge. Until this policy is changed, there will continue to be tragic outcomes.

## TO THE EDITOR OF THE RECORD:

## The Terrible Mistake in Pima County

J. Eric Fuller, one of the shooting victims of the Tucson tragedy, was involuntarily committed for mental health evaluation after he spoke threateningly at a televised forum on the tragedy. Jared Loughner, who for three years displayed bizarre and irrational, if not overtly psychotic behavior, was merely required to obtain psychiatric clearance before he could resume his college studies. We now know that this was tragic mistake. Judging by reports of Loughner's behavior in the press, there were many indications for involuntary psychiatric evaluation. In the case of Mr. Fuller, it only took one.

## TO THE EDITOR OF THE NEW YORK TIMES:

## The Prevalence of Mental Illness

The results of the study of the prevalence of mental illness as reported in "Most Will be Mentally Ill at Some Point, Study Says" (Tuesday, June 7, 2005, p. A18) are no surprise to me. As a psychiatrist, I have seen many patients respond to treatment for a major depressive episode only to then report that they feel even better than before and realize they were depressed for many years, if not all their lives. Some even suspect that they would have done more with their lives if they had had treatment earlier for the 'emotional ups and downs' which they never realized were treatable symptoms. This has come to the attention of the medical profession recently, and attempts are being made to remedy the situation. The unfortunate fact that psychological evaluation is rarely a part of routine physical examinations is due mainly to the inexperience of general practitioners in the evaluation of psychiatric conditions. Time constraints dictated by low insurance reimbursements for these services also make it impossible to delve deeply into a patient's history and correctly assess symptoms of emotional discomfort.

## Schizophrenia, a Devastating Brain Disease

Mr. Cho, the perpetrator of the tragic mass killings at Virginia Tech, was in all probability suffering from chronic paranoid schizophrenia. It is a shame that so little is understood by the public about severe mental illness other than that some people are 'crazy.' Schizophrenia, the most severe, devastating and disabling of the psychoses, is an inherited, organic brain disease affecting people in all societies worldwide. It is what used to fill the state mental hospitals before the discovery of the highly effective antipsychotic medications which physicians now have at their disposal and which made it possible to reduce the population in New York State mental hospitals from over 90,000 to less than 10,000. Schizophrenia causes a break with reality and is characterized by delusions, hallucinations, disorganized thinking and overwhelming impulses over which the person affected has little or no control. We have all read of mothers who kill their children because the voice of God told them to do so. Can you imagine having an illness that could do that to you? Fortunately, pharmacological treatment can eliminate most symptoms of schizophrenia, and persons with the disease can live something very much like normal and productive lives if they receive the proper medications. Hopefully this disaster will increase the public's desire for more knowledge and understanding of the disease and will help remove the stigma attached to severe mental illness.

In the ongoing discussion in the press and media about why the heartbreaking disaster at Virginia Tech happened, little mention is made of the role played by current stringent mental health laws championed by the ACLU. At present, a person can only be hospitalized involuntarily if they are determined to be dangerous. Making this determination is both difficult and unreliable, with the result that most mentally ill people, even if they are severely ill, cannot be forced into hospital treatment. In the past, a person could be hospitalized involuntarily if they were determined to be suffering from a psychosis. If that criterion had still been in effect, not only would Mr. Cho probably have been placed in a hospital and given treatment, so would the 300,000 mentally ill Americans who are currently in prison, untreated and mistreated, and the many thousands living untreated on the streets of our cities.

Paradoxically, now that we have the ability to offer people with major psychoses highly effective treatment, they are systematically deprived of treatment and left to fend for themselves on the street or else land in jail for some minor offense. The tragedy at Virginia Tech is only the most dramatic, visible and shocking consequence of our misguided mental health laws which only guarantee that the most vulnerable members of society are ignored, cast out or maltreated. Dorothy Dix, where are you now?

# Chapter 2

# SOME THOUGHTS ON PSYCHOANALYSIS

THE HISTORY OF PSYCHOTHERAPY IN the United States began in the 1920s and 1930s with the introduction and establishment of psychoanalysis. Up to that point there had been 'common sense' psychiatry, which had little of the dynamism of most later disciplines in the field. Psychoanalysis, meanwhile, was the first attempt at a formalized therapeutic procedure based on a systematic psychological theory, namely, that developed by Sigmund Freud in the latter part of the 19th century. It also had some features of a belief system and comprised an elaborate set of theoretical constructs and a therapeutic technique which purported to uncover the unconscious origins of psychological experiences, impulses and behavior. It was felt that this exploration would lead to experiential and behavioral changes in the subject—the so-called analysand.

Although psychoanalysis had originated in Europe, it never really caught on there in the way it did later in the U.S. As the Nazis came to power in Germany in the 1930s, a large number of analysts and those interested in the field, many of them Jewish, emigrated to America. The first psychoanalytic institute was established in the early 1930s in New York City.

Psychoanalysis became quite popular in its adopted homeland. It was new and innovative and it delved more deeply into the human psyche than anything had before. It was popularized in the culture through plays such as *Lady in the Dark*, movies such as *Spellbound* (in which Ingrid Bergman played analyst to Gregory Peck's patient), novels, etc. At first it attracted mainly people interested in psychological research, a highly intellectual crowd interested in the theory more than its therapeutic applications. Dr. Phyllis Greenleaf, the president of the NY Psychoanalytic Institute in the 1940s, once told beginning analytic students that they should see themselves first and foremost as "true researchers" and not as therapists. In fact, many of the early 'orthodox' analysts took the position that it could not be their concern whether the analysand got better or not; their task was to analyze the subject's 'free associations' and interpret their unconscious meaning. According to this view, what the analysand did with that knowledge and insight would depend on his or her own ego integration. The process was essentially an investigative one, the aim of which was to make the unconscious conscious, thereby enabling subjects to integrate this knowledge into their psychology and, hopefully but not necessarily, experience greater adjustment and gratification in their lives.

Some psychoanalysts at the time defined the process in quite limited and pedantic terms. One author in the 1950s defined psychoanalysis as "that procedure in which an attempt is made to develop a transference neurosis in the patient and resolve this neurosis by interpretation alone. Anything else is not analysis." Much has changed since then. Psychoanalysis early on came to focus its attention on the whole area of ego defense mechanisms, thereby opening new doors for the exploration and analysis of the transference neurosis. Since then, the field has evolved in a wide variety of innovative directions. A number of different analytical schools broke away from the original orthodoxy of the New York Psychoanalytic Society to go on and develop their own analytical theories and procedures.

One factor leading to this separation and diversification was that the availability of classical analysis was greatly limited by several factors. First, the number of trained analysts itself was limited, since the analytic schools could produce only a few each year. There was therefore usually a long waiting list for anyone seeking analytic therapy. Second, the treatment was time-consuming, involving daily sessions over a period of several years and requiring a substantial financial investment. For these reasons, psychoanalysis was out of reach for most people.

Meanwhile, and despite these practical obstacles, the number of psychiatrists interested in the field continued to grow. It was these professionals who over the years went on to develop a whole series of other psychotherapies. At first these were based on psychoanalytic theories and concepts. Later on, newer and more original theories and therapeutic modalities appeared, including interactional therapy, transactional therapy, client-centered therapy, behavioral therapy, hypnoanalytic therapy and, more recently, cognitive behavioral therapy, just to name a few. The most popular of these, usually referred to as psychoanalytically oriented psychotherapies or dynamic therapies, incorporate elements of analytic theory but do not confine treatment to daily on-the-couch sessions with psychoanalytic interpretation. The particular techniques used often vary from therapist to therapist.

The central element in classical psychoanalytic treatment is the development and interpretation of the transference, that is, the projection by the patient of a fantasy onto the analyst. This is usually a recreation of the patient's infantile and/or childhood relationship with parents or siblings. One speaks of a father or mother transference, which can be further described as negative, positive, idealized, erotic, dependent, passive, etc. It is the process of developing these distorted projections into the therapeutic situation that provides the material for understanding the history of the patient's development in the family. It also provides an opportunity for the analyst to offer insights into the patient's way of relating to the analyst that are supposed to have relevance for the patient's way of relating to others in his or her life. It is believed that understanding and gaining insight into the transference should be therapeutic, that is, it should help the patient become better adjusted in their relationships with other people and recognize mental distortions that interfere with these relationships. The handling of the transference and the objective of resolving it are the essential characteristics of psychoanalytic therapy.

The heyday of psychoanalysis was in the 1940s, 50s and 60s. Since that time its popularity has declined, and less ambitious, more accessible and more therapy-oriented psychotherapies have offered analytic insights to a wider patient population. There is still a sizeable number of psychoanalysts in practice and one can still receive the traditional 'couch' treatment. Many analysts, however, have given up the orthodox approach and have found that less demanding and dogmatic approaches to treatment can be just as therapeutically effective, if not more so. In fact, some modifications of the traditional analytic approach are highly effective.

A large number of the would-be analysts in the early years who could not be accommodated at the traditional analytic institutes found as they explored other options that they were more interested in therapy than theory. Their goals were aimed more at symptom relief, and an extensive literature developed around approaches that were based on psychoanalytic theories but in which the therapeutic procedure was largely modified. The treatment format of once or twice weekly sessions of vis-à-vis therapy (face-to-face conversation between therapist and patient) has become far more prevalent than the couch of traditional analysis, and some prominent analysts consider it just as effective. Nevertheless, one still occasionally reads articles in the general press about traditional psychoanalysis, and the following letters were written in response to such articles.

\* \* \*

## TO THE EDITOR OF NEW YORK MAGAZINE:

Your recent article on psychoanalysis (October 16, 1997) could have been written in the 1950s. That was the heyday of psychoanalysis in our culture. Moss Hart's *Lady in the Dark* was on Broadway and Ingrid Bergman played Gregory Peck's analyst in the movie *Spellbound*. Analyzing dreams was all the rage, and psychoanalysts had year-long waiting lists.

There had been a large influx of big names in the field from Europe, and New York had replaced Old World capitals as the new center of the analytic movement. Unfortunately, however, the emphasis in the field was on theoretical studies of Freud's ideas. That is, psychoanalysts were more interested in the procedure than the patient. In fact, to this day no scientific evidence has ever been presented that psychoanalysis is an effective treatment for any psychiatric disorder, or, for that matter, that it ever cured anyone of anything! No doubt many patients have been helped in their self-understanding and adjustment to life, but even that assertion is only based on anecdotal, not scientific evidence.

Psychoanalysis was, in effect, a belief system—what I would call the 'religion of genitality.' Freud's libido theory defined the early stages of psychological development as oral, anal, phallic, latency and genital, the latter being the most mature. Anything 'pre-genital' was considered sin, with the worst sin of all being narcissism. Analyses went on interminably, as Freud himself admitted in a paper entitled *Analysis Terminable and Interminable*. Analysts defended themselves against that charge using the circular logic characteristic of closed systems: when something went well for an analysand, it was thanks to the analysis; when things went poorly, it was due to the patient's resistance. This served as an all-encompassing rationalization for therapeutic failure. Analysts even coined the term 'negative therapeutic reaction,' which was a euphemism meaning that the patient got worse as a result of the treatment instead of better. This failure was then blamed on the patient's way of communicating with the analyst. Rarely did an analyst admit being unable to understand and therefore unable to help a patient; or that the analyst's own negative transference reaction to a patient was hampering treatment and the patient ought to see someone else; or that analysis in some cases simply did not work. In fact the opposite was true; early analysts acted for all the world as if their knowledge came directly from divinely inspired sources and was therefore unassailable. Perhaps after putting so much time and effort into the rigorous training it was difficult to question its value and be objective about its therapeutic usefulness. (Be that as it may, even traditional analysts now suggest that after three years of analysis a review be done to see if there is a counter-transferential problem, that is, a negative unconscious emotional reaction in the analyst that may be interfering with progress.)

Early on, psychoanalysts viewed other therapies with condescension and ridicule, as impurities that could only contaminate the pure gold of analysis. The arguments they used to defend themselves are reminiscent of those used by religious groups. Not surprisingly, the three leading analytic theorists of the day were known as 'the holy Trinity' and the New York Psychoanalytic Institute as the 'orthodox' school. Now, apparently, even some of the old-timers, as they near the end of their careers and don't have quite so much to lose, are coming out and saying that much less intensive psychotherapy with vis-à-vis sessions once or twice a week is just as effective as the traditional format of daily sessions on the couch. Analysts are now also admitting that they can't actually identify the factors on which therapeutic effectiveness depends, and that other therapies and less analytically indoctrinated therapists are able to get comparable results. (God forbid that social workers could be just as effective therapists as analysts!) I have even heard some experienced classical analysts say that they now think using the couch is actually counter-therapeutic! An experienced analyst colleague once voiced his opinion quite concisely and cogently: "Psychoanalysis is a good psychological education for a healthy person who can afford it"! (This is the closest thing I have ever heard to a complete and accurate definition of analysis.)

A former president of the American Psychoanalytic Association once presented a case of his own at a scientific meeting which he himself was chairing. He reported that after having analyzed a patient for two years he still didn't know whether the patient was schizophrenic or not. To this I would say that, in the first place, psychoanalysis is not the appropriate treatment for schizophrenia; and secondly, anyone who can't make a diagnosis of schizophrenia after two years of daily sessions shouldn't be practicing psychiatry. This is just one example showing how stubbornly the analytic community has resisted the accepted opinion of most psychiatrists that schizophrenia is an organic disease of the brain.

That said, there is still no doubt that Freud's discoveries and the psychoanalytic movement with its many insights were revolutionary in their day. More than any other theory they formed the basis of, and have had immeasurable influence on, the development of modern psychiatry and the way we treat patients today.

## TO THE EDITOR OF THE NEW YORK TIMES:

In "Therapists Go Crazy for One in Sopranos" (December 29, 2001, p. A13) I was both puzzled and pleasantly surprised to read that psychoanalysts have embraced the character of Dr. Melfi as one of their own, with what the author refers to as "dangerously warm feelings, tinged with envy, gratitude, pride and confusion, etc." It should be pointed out though, that what the Sopranos' Dr. Melfi practices is not traditional psychoanalysis. That would usually involve five sessions a week conducted with the patient lying on a couch and without the aid of psychotropic medications. What she practices is called insight or dynamic psychotherapy, which, though based somewhat on psychoanalytic theory, is done seated vis-à-vis and often involves psychopharmacology. Up until the not-too-distant past, analysts themselves made a clear distinction between *psychoanalysis*—in their view the gold standard—and *psychotherapy*, an alloy which they viewed not without a tinge of contempt. And as for medications, that was a strong *no-no* in psychoanalysis. The idea was that it was desirable that the analysand should experience some discomfort in order to keep motivated for the difficult task of analysis. I have even heard analysts say they did not want to 'experiment' with the newer psychotropic medications such as Prozac, Zoloft, and Serzone! (We now know that these medications, along with psychotherapy, can bring about therapeutic results and characterological changes comparable to and even more effective than those achievable with prolonged psychoanalytic treatment.) It sounds to me like there certainly is both envy and confusion in the psychoanalytic community these days—and it appears that once-clear distinctions have been substantially blurred.

## TO THE EDITOR OF THE NEW YORK TIMES:

In your article on a get-together of psychoanalysts (March 14, 1998, p. B9), one pre-eminent analyst in the field is quoted as saying, "We are experts not in helping patients learn facts but in helping them construct myths. We are fantasy doctors, not reality doctors. We don't help patients decide what is true. It's important to show them that they can organize their experience in many ways, that they can become more comfortable not about what happened in the past but about uncertainty and ambiguity. We are experts at helping patients with these impossible epistemological problems."

In other words, he seems to be saying, psychoanalysts are *con artists.* No wonder psychoanalysis doesn't work! In the old days, the traditional analysis based on libido theory consisted of fitting the patient into predetermined theoretical constructs not to help the patient but in order to confirm the correctness of the constructs. If the analysand failed to accept an interpretation, it was seen as 'resistance.' This was necessary in order for analysts to maintain the conviction that they were right. They worked with psychoanalytic theory as if it were something handed down from on high, the central text of a religion centered around the almighty genitalia. Analysts paid almost exclusive attention to what they viewed as the closed system of the patient's internal mental life, showing little interest in what had happened in the family to influence the patient in his or her development. (Many psychiatrists, upon realizing that that didn't work, abandoned traditional psychotherapy and began to take an interest in family dynamics and develop family therapies.)

According to the analyst quoted in the article, the truth about a patient's past life experience should be of no interest to either analyst or patient. This, to me, is the height of therapeutic nihilism and misses entirely what psychotherapy is all about. Instead of helping a patient to feel better, the analysts replaces one set of fantasies, the patient's, with another set of fantasies more to the analyst's liking, based on the assumption that the analyst's guess about what happened is better than the patient's. In essence, the analyst is saying, "Let me tell you what fantasies you should believe." What a narcissistic view of the doctor-patient relationship! What guruism!

Contrast this with the useful and productive notion that we are all living out our childhood traumas. The biblical adage "Seek ye the truth and the truth shall set you free" says it all. In my opinion, this is the *sine qua non* of good psychotherapy. The only way for a patient to achieve real understanding and useful insight is to come as close as possible to learning the truth about what went on in his or her earlier development. Only then can one decide what part one's own reaction played in the development of one's defenses and life patterns; only then can one become free to see and experience oneself as one really is, uncolored by earlier identities.

Traditional analysts, who put all the onus for psychic dysfunction on the patient's flawed ego, are reluctant to side with the patient or give support and encouragement during the therapeutic process. Meanwhile, it is exceedingly therapeutic for a patient to learn that his or her seemingly pathological reaction as a child to stresses within the family was in fact healthy, a sign of strength under difficult circumstances, and not evidence of inadequacy or abnormality. In my opinion, recovering and establishing the truth of what actually happened in a patient's life is essential for a successful therapeutic outcome. Maybe instead of being "fantasy doctors," analysts should try for once being "reality doctors" like the rest of us in the mental health profession. They might like it—and it might work!


## TO THE EDITOR OF PSYCHIATRIC NEWS:

The recent article "Psychoanalysts Rally to Ensure Future of Embattled Specialty" highlights a major change in the perception and importance of psychoanalysis within the field of psychiatry.

Certainly in the so-called heyday of analysis there was wide acceptance of the procedure. As the article pointed out, World War II generated increased interest in psychiatry and many doctors returning from the war went into that specialty. Psychoanalysis had a good image in popular culture as well, appearing at its most glamorous in the movie *Spellbound*, where none other than Ingrid Bergman played psychoanalyst to Gregory Peck's patient.

Analysis was popular, analysts had long waiting lists and psychiatric residents vied for admission to a handful of small, highly competitive analytic institutes. That was the heyday of psychoanalysis.

Meanwhile, it turns out that belief in the efficacy of analysis is based entirely on anecdotal evidence. Certainly analysis could never meet the FDA's rigorous requirements for a treatment procedure, since it has never been proven safe and effective. (Suicide by analysands is not unknown; there have been a number of prominent cases.) Apparently there was an attempt to study the effectiveness of analysis in the 1950s but the results were suppressed and never published, apparently for the reason that it might "undermine the faith of analysands."

Psychoanalysts have long considered their procedure sacrosanct. One prominent and well-published analyst recently declared that "any therapy other than analysis is bullshit." When asked where he got his analytic patients these days, he replied "I make them into analytic patients." That, in a nutshell, is the problem: psychoanalysts are more interested in defending and maintaining the purity of their procedure than they are in offering patients what they need, i.e., the most effective treatment.

Recently I ran into a well-known and widely published analyst on the street and in the course of our conversation he opined, "Those old training analyses were no good." He was referring to the requirement that analysts in training themselves undergo analysis by senior analysts. The training analyst had enormous power to affect a trainee's status at an institute and therefore his or her career. Naturally enough, it was felt by some that the trainee analysand could not possibly be fully spontaneous under such circumstances, and that a satisfactory examination of his or her unconscious was therefore impossible. And yet despite this, many analytic candidates were disqualified from further training by their training analyst, in some cases after many years of analysis.

The orthodox schools were so obsessive in their adherence to doctrine that they would brook no opposition to or doubting of their dogma, much like an orthodox religion. In my opinion, the main reason why analysis lost its popularity is that its practitioners remained more committed to the procedure than to patients' needs. One finds, for instance, that analysts do not relate to patients as people; in fact, they rarely called their own patients by their actual names. It is not uncommon after several years of unsuccessful analysis for a patient to be referred to another analyst for 'reanalysis.' One prominent analyst once said that only if she was doing a reanalysis would she generally call the analysand by name, since she felt that the repeated and prolonged emotional distancing was counterproductive. (She was right!)

Another well-known analyst once told me that he hated to admit it, but to his surprise antidepressants seemed to cure phobias. When I asked him why he hated to admit it he said "because most of my analytic practice is phobias!" (It is indeed true that the newer medications, such as selective serotonin reuptake inhibitors, SSRIs, have revolutionized the treatment of many disorders.)

The article makes it clear that analysts are first and foremost interested in doing what they have always done rather than looking for ways to make treatment more effective, relevant and worth the time and money spent on it by the patient. In fact, psychoanalysts have never referred to analysis as therapy, and many analysts say they make no claims for its therapeutic effect. Some even say that the only way they can do real analysis is if they don't care whether the patient gets better or not! They then rationalize this attitude by claiming that if the analyst cared about patient outcomes it would undermine his or her objectivity and possibly cause negative counter-transference in the event the patient didn't respond well to treatment. Another prominent analyst once said that the practice of psychoanalysis should continue unchanged even if it was demonstrated to be ineffective as treatment!

The reality is that new SSRIs and their cousins have indeed brought new treatment possibilities to the field. In my experience, psychoanalysts may give lip service to such medications and on occasion use them, but they do not make efforts to become knowledgeable about their use. I have seen cases in which therapeutic results were achieved using Zoloft that were entirely comparable to those typically requiring several years of analysis—not only symptomatic changes, but real characterological changes that remain evident in long-term follow-up. These include dramatic changes in cases involving self-esteem issues, passive aggression, masochistic personality disorders, addictions, social phobias, etc. Certainly, in most cases such medications are best used in conjunction with psychotherapy, but even then treatment is much shorter and much more effective than years of analysis.

The jokes around Woody Allen's having been in analysis for 19 years are sad. My only comment is that his treatment was, to say the least, ineffective. I have known of other people who were in analysis for many years without success. The usual explanation from analysts for such failures is that there was too much resistance on the part of the patient or that something happened too early in the patient's life—never that the analysis was ineffective or that it might have been the analyst's fault.

## TO THE EDITOR OF THE NEW YORK TIMES:

## Psychoanalysis and Psychotherapy—They're Not the Same Thing

In "Calling All Ids: Freudians Fight a Turf War" (May 29, 2004, p. B7) the question is asked "Is there a real difference between analysis and analytic psychotherapy?" There most definitely is a difference. Psychoanalysis, as developed by Freud, essentially seeks to explore unconscious psychodynamics and make them conscious through the exclusive use of its only form of intervention, interpretation. That alone, and not the alleviation of symptoms or curing of a disorder, is its stated goal. Psychotherapy, on the other hand, including forms of psychotherapy that are based on psychoanalysis, is essentially goal-oriented and utilizes a variety of interventions, such as support, reassurance, behavior modification and suggestion, as well as the newer cognitive approaches. Its goals include relieving symptoms, improving self-esteem and changing behavior.

Numerous clinical studies have shown various psychotherapeutic techniques to be effective in treating specific psychiatric disorders, especially in combination with the new generation of psychotropic medications. Analysts do analysis; psychotherapists do psychotherapy. They are not trying to do the same thing, and consequently they do not accomplish the same thing.

As Lawrence Kubie, a highly regarded and oft-quoted psychoanalyst, once observed much to the dismay of his fellow analysts, "What most analysands need is some good psychotherapy." He was a strong proponent of analysts doing a thorough psychiatric evaluation of every prospective analysand, including family history and other details of the patient's life. Unfortunately, this never became the usual procedure in analytic circles.

## TO THE EDITOR OF THE NEW YORK TIMES:

### She Didn't Want to Be Shrunk

As a practicing psychiatrist who uses both psychotherapy and pharmacology, both alone and in combination, I read Ms. Merkin's "I'm Shrunk" (Magazine Section, Sunday, August 8, 2010) with particular interest. To my mind, the obvious conclusion to draw from the story of the patient who was in various sorts of analysis over a period of 40 years, and from the case of Woody Allen, who was allegedly in analysis for 19 years, is that analysis doesn't work! A prominent psychoanalyst is quoted in the article as saying that patients need support and love and that that is not compatible with the analytic process. I agree that that is what patients need, but they also specifically need some of the things they didn't get early in their lives, including an understanding of how their early life circumstances still influence their thinking, self-image and behavior. There are people for whom neither analysis nor psychotherapy are the right thing; the author seems to belong to this group. Perhaps she would have done better in group therapy, which is more supportive and family-like. The fact that she cites as her model Elaine May, who got her analyst to divorce his wife and marry her (!), indicates that the author was actually looking for something other than therapy, namely, a real relationship with an ideal parent. This, I suspect, is what she was looking for and wasn't able to find in all the therapists she saw over the course of 40 years until she finally gave up looking. She wasn't at all looking for a therapist, in fact; as she says herself, ever since she was young she had been looking for someone who would reparent her. Unable to let go of that wish, she couldn't help but be disappointed with psychotherapy as a way to help her get through the rest of her life as an adult.

## TO THE EDITOR OF NEWSWEEK:

### A Shrink Talks Back

As a practicing psychiatrist I found much to object to in Sharon Begley's "Get Shrunk at Your Own Risk" (Newsweek, June 18, p. 49). In the first place, the title is grossly inappropriate and demeaning to mental health professionals. Calling us headshrinkers, even in jest, is unacceptable and only plays into the lingering stigma associated with psychological treatment. I doubt the author would have entitled an article about ineffective or botched surgery "Get Butchered at Your Own Risk." She also makes disparaging comments about antipsychotic medications, but she should have been around before they existed, as I was, when all we had for schizophrenic patients was electroconvulsive (shock) therapy, insulin coma therapy and trans-orbital and frontal lobotomy. None of these treatments came even close to what modern medications can do—not to speak of the side effects! The newer antidepressants do have their side effects, but believe me, they can also turn people's lives around. They are truly, in my opinion, miracle drugs. I call them brain normalizers. No doubt there are some inexperienced psychotherapists using unorthodox treatments who should be more closely monitored, but that is no reason to question the value and effectiveness of a whole class of highly effective psychotherapeutic and pharmacological treatments that are at our disposal. As for Ms. Begley's comments about dissociative identity disorder, it should be pointed out that this is an area that has received too little attention and presents problems that not many therapists have had experience handling. It may well be that some resort to untested, innovative methods in an attempt to reach these patients, who are notoriously very difficult to work with. In fact, the only chance for such patients to find treatment may be with inventive and pioneering therapists who are willing to stick their necks out and try new and unproven techniques. Her assertion however that 10%-20% percent of all patients who receive psychotherapy are harmed is way out of line. If I found that this was happening in my practice, I would quit tomorrow! (The figures cited sound more like the percentage of patients who are *not helped*, rather than the percentage harmed.)

## TO THE EDITOR OF PSYCHIATRIC TIMES:

## Borderline Personality Disorder

The interesting article "Psychodynamic Psychotherapy for Borderline Personality Disorder" (Psychiatric Times, July, 2004, p. 53) begins with "There is no place for the analyst as a blank screen onto which patients project their internal fantasies." In my opinion, there is no place for this in any type of psychotherapy, not only classical psychoanalysis. I think that this, in fact, is the reason psychoanalysis never lived up to theoretical expectations regarding its therapeutic effectiveness. Certainly analysis has never been shown clinically to be an effective treatment for any psychiatric disorder. When I was a resident, the head of the department, a well-known analyst, used to say that he could only analyze if he didn't care whether the patient got well or not. Other analysts I have known have confirmed that this, essentially, is the analytic stance. The rationale for this position seems to be that, if the patient senses the analyst's vested interest in a cure, he or she might act out an infantile negative transference—or some other unconscious dynamic—and 'refuse' to get better.

Analysts of yore felt that adopting a detached, supposedly objective position was necessary in order to remove any interpersonal relationship from the therapeutic equation. This was gross denial. What they didn't realize was that there was, indeed, often a very strong interpersonal relationship, except that in the analyst it was unconscious and was referred to as 'counter-transference' when it appeared. It not infrequently erupted in the form of sexual encounters with analysands, as well as actual marriages, both of which often resulted in unpleasant or disastrous outcomes.

At the end of the article, after a very sophisticated and detailed theoretical discussion, there appears the sentence, "The skill, experience, attitudes and interpersonal ability of the psychiatrist or other mental health care professional may be as important as the type of therapy, particularly because treatment of personality disorders relies on an interpersonal process." My response is: Isn't this the case in all psychotherapy? As Eric Kandel of Columbia Medical School once said, "Psychotherapy is the neuronal activity of one person acting on the neuronal activity of another."

## TO THE EDITOR OF THE NEW YORK TIMES:

## Surgery as Therapy

In "Surgery as Therapy" (Sunday Review, August 14, 2011, p. 12) we learn of a young Brazilian woman who wanted a breast implant because, as she says, "I didn't want to put in an implant to exhibit myself, but to feel better. It wasn't simple vanity, but a necessary vanity. Surgery improves a woman's auto-estima." The prominent plastic surgeon quoted says his "humanistic approach to medicine includes the healing potential of surgery: self-esteem." He argues that "the real object of healing is not the body, but the mind. A plastic surgeon is a 'psychologist with a scalpel.'" Speaking of plastic and reconstructive surgery, he says that "in both types of surgery beauty and mental healing mingle—and both benefit health." Another doctor—jokingly, he admitted—asked "What is the difference between a plastic surgeon and a psychoanalyst? Answer: The psychoanalyst knows everything and changes nothing. The plastic surgeon knows nothing, but changes everything."

Apparently psychological treatment, including psychoanalysis, is quite popular in Brazil because there is no stigma attached, and plastic surgery is popular because people give a high priority to personal appearance.

# Chapter 3

# DEPRESSION

Clinical depression is one of the most common medical conditions affecting people in our society. A person need not be sad in order to be diagnosed with depression. There are many symptoms that are more important, both for diagnosis and for treatment: indifference to one's usual interests, reduced energy, loss of appetite, disturbed sleep (especially waking early in the morning), loss of weight, withdrawal from social contact, irritability, loss of memory, weakened concentration and low self-esteem. A depressed mood (sadness) is also present in most cases, but not always. Although most depressive disorders are highly treatable through psychotherapy and medications, it is estimated that only about 25% of sufferers ever seek and receive treatment. The rest are told by family members to cheer up because they have nothing to be depressed about—hearing this advice actually tends to make the depression worse—or else they themselves view their depression as a sign of a weak character instead of the treatable condition it is.

\*   \*   \*

## TO THE EDITOR OF THE NEW YORK TIMES:

What a surprise it was for me to read Maureen Dowd's flippant, know-it-all, wise-ass column (June 10, 2001) on a subject about which she knows practically nothing! I am ashamed of her and you can tell her I said so! Her columns are usually witty, insightful and amusing, but this one is mostly just reveals her ignorance and does a disservice to those who suffer from serious psychological disorders and have found amazing relief from the new generation of psychotropic drugs.

Freud himself predicted that the next major breakthrough in psychiatric treatment would come from the field of biochemistry. Well, he was right, and this has already happened. Certainly there are abuses in the prescription of these miracle drugs, and I agree with Ms. Dowd regarding the overprescribing of Prozac and Ritalin to children, many of whom are really crying out for more contact with their overworked, multitasking mothers. I myself have referred to these drugs as the new mothers of America. Their use to treat adults, however, is different. These new medications are referred to as antidepressants, but I prefer to call them brain normalizers because that is exactly what they do: they restore normal neuronal activity in the brain. Patients do not feel like they are on 'uppers'; they feel normal. The results that can be achieved with these medications are comparable to the best results achievable with years of daily, on-the-couch sessions with a psychoanalyst.

Depression is the most underdiagnosed and undertreated condition in our society, especially in men, who hesitate to seek psychiatric help or may not even know they are clinically depressed. Meanwhile, treatment can be very effective, for both women and men, even for those suffering from lifelong depression or other psychological disorders or impediments. Whether symptomatic or characterological, these disorders, which can seriously interfere with occupational achievement and interpersonal relationships and are often accompanied by severe psychic pain, are eminently treatable. In the past, many patients were not helped by analysis or psychotherapy or the earlier generation of medications, and there is therefore a tendency to ignore or underestimate the real improvements that have been made in treatment modalities. In fact, it has been proven that these newer medications, in conjunction with some form of psychotherapeutic intervention, are very effective and have few side effects. I have seen them bring about real changes in the character, personality and behavior of patients that could be considered life-changing and in some cases life-saving.

If Ms. Dowd insists on making "sweeping generalizations" (her words) about medical matters, she should rely less on anecdotal evidence and more on the latest scientific literature.

## TO THE EDITOR OF THE NEW YORK TIMES:

Since you chose not to publish my first letter criticizing Maureen Dowd's outrageous op-ed piece (Sunday June 10, 2001), I am writing again to ask why the Times regularly publishes columns by a person who would refer to people with emotional disorders as "crazy," "nuts," "wacko-bango" and "loony"? Is this your idea of good journalism on the subject of psychiatric problems? Everyone knows that psychiatric medications are being overprescribed, but is this a serious attempt to focus on the problem? Or is it Ms. Dowd's attempt to be funny? If so, she fails miserably. I think she should be called on this and the Times should issue some sort of an apology.

## TO THE EDITOR OF THE NEW YORK TIMES:

You reported recently that the death of White House counsel Vincent Foster was now considered a suicide and not the result of some ominous conspiracy, as had been hinted in the past. A physician was quoted as saying that Mr. Foster had a mental disorder which had been undertreated. Alas, this is all too often the case. Depression is one of the most common illnesses in our society, and yet it continues to be one of the most misunderstood, underdiagnosed, and undertreated of all medical conditions. Depression also lies at the root of many physical illnesses, most notably back problems, which are very common and for which most sufferers mistakenly go to orthopedic specialists rather than psychiatrists. Masked depression is behind a long list of other physical complaints and illnesses and can take other forms as well, including various extreme behaviors. It has recently been shown that depression is the most reliable predictor of heart attack and is therefore perhaps the leading cause of premature death in our country. Countless deaths could be avoided if we could overcome our blindness to this ubiquitous affliction.

However, as with other emotional illnesses, depressive disorders still carry the stigma of being a sign of weak character in the sufferer. It is especially taboo—almost unthinkable—for people in high places to be seen as having any kind of emotional illness. Ill-informed and inconsiderate relatives all too often tell the depressed person to "snap out of it." This makes about as much sense as telling someone to snap out of measles or diabetes. In fact, such callous advice only serves to make the depression worse by dumping a load of guilt on the sufferer and increasing their feelings of inadequacy.

Unfortunately, our society, including the medical profession, has still not gotten the message about depression. We need to deal with it as the very common, painful and often totally disabling disorder that it is and steer victims to the right professional for treatment as early as possible. Depression is now a highly treatable condition for which we have amazingly effective medications and psychotherapeutic techniques.

## TO THE EDITOR OF THE NEW YORK TIMES:

Today's article by Dr. Sally Satel (June 10, 2005) undermines the very timely and much needed landmark science-based report by Surgeon General David Satcher on mental illness in the United States. At a time when the treatment of the mentally ill is in such a sad state, Dr. Satel's main concern seems to be doing whatever costs the least! Her article will only serve to reinforce unproductive attitudes toward this serious problem. Prevention and early detection are essential parts of dealing with any serious medical issue. Support systems and "objective friends," contrary to her assertion, cannot perform psychiatric evaluations and diagnose and treat mental disorders. To follow her suggestions would quite literally set us back decades in the treatment of mental illness. Instead, the Surgeon General's report and its recommendations deserve to be fully supported by all psychiatrists.

In the first place, depression is one of the most underdiagnosed and undertreated medical conditions in our society. There are a number of reasons why this is so. First, the stigma and shame associated with consulting a psychiatrist continue to discourage patients from seeking help early, as do the admonitions of friends and relatives that one should simply pull oneself together and get on with life, which amounts to saying that one should pull oneself up by one's own bootstraps. When early symptoms are played down in this way, the opportunity for early detection and treatment aimed at preventing more serious illness is lost. Instead we should be supporting the program currently being developed by the American Psychiatric Association to train general practitioners to detect depression early so they can refer patients for appropriate psychiatric evaluation and treatment. Insurance companies still haven't come to realize that making psychiatric services more readily available would actually leverage an enormous reduction in the use of other, far more expensive medical services. By trivializing this far-reaching problem and undermining the Surgeon General's report, Dr. Satel does a great disservice to people suffering from depression and to society at large. Her view is from the ivory tower of a think-tank, not the front lines of clinical medicine.

# TO THE EDITOR OF THE NEW YORK TIMES:

## Depression, a Disease of the Brain

I see in "Your Zoloft Might Prevent a Heart Attack" an encouraging sign that the medical community and society in general are getting the message that depression is a disease of the brain. Psychoanalysts and psychologists have long resisted this idea and as a consequence have disparaged the use of psychotropic medications for the treatment of depression. In fact, in a letter to the editor published in the same edition of the Times, a psychologist opines that "depression is a psychological disorder, not a medical illness." This clinician obviously doesn't know much about brain physiology and neurochemistry, in particular that all mental functioning is accompanied by neuronal activity, e.g. neurotransmitter activity of neurons. Even psychotherapy has been described by Eric Kandel of Columbia University as the neuronal activity of one person (the therapist) acting on the neuronal activity of another (the patient). Freud himself said that he was studying only the *psychology* of the brain and that the next big advance in our understanding of human behavior would come from the study of brain *anatomy and physiology.* That time has come, and clinical studies have shown that the optimal treatment for most psychiatric disorders is psychotherapy accompanied by the right medication.

# TO THE EDITOR OF THE NEW YORK TIMES:

## When Sadness Is a Good Thing

The author of "When Sadness Is a Good Thing" tries to make the point that psychiatrists overdiagnose and overmedicate people who are simply experiencing normal feelings associated with life's stresses. Some psychiatrists may well be guilty of this, but not knowledgeable ones. Sadness alone in a patient is in any case not enough to make a diagnosis of either neurotic depression (now called dysthymia) or major depression. The far larger problem, in fact, is that vast numbers of people—the majority—suffering from real clinical depression are undiagnosed and/or undertreated. Unfortunately, general practitioners as a rule are not experienced in diagnosing clinical depression, so their depressed patients never get referred to a psychiatrist. In actual depression, incidentally, sadness may not even be present. The important clinical symptoms of depression are: poor concentration, slowed thinking, indecisiveness, poor appetite with weight loss, persistent early morning awakening, low energy, fatigue, lack of interest, inability to enjoy oneself, social withdrawal, lowered self-esteem, irritability and, sometimes, suicidal thoughts. Cases such as those mentioned by the author involving unusual sadness owing to loss, disappointment or other stresses would most likely be correctly diagnosed, according to DSM-IV, as 'adjustment reaction with depressed mood.' Patients with this diagnosis generally respond to psychotherapy or counseling alone without any sort of medication. Normal mourning, on the other hand, is in itself not an indication for any sort of psychiatric intervention.

## TO THE EDITOR OF PSYCHIATRIC ANNALS:

This weekend I attended the Psychiatric Annals symposium on anxiety disorders at the New York Hilton. Numerous clinical studies were presented assessing the efficacy of various psychotropic medications compared with placebos. As one lecturer pointed out, most studies show that medications are about 20% more effective than placebos. Psychotherapy as a treatment modality was conspicuous by its absence, having hardly been mentioned by any of the presenters. When I asked one why this was the case, he opined that clinical studies of psychotherapy were too difficult to do because there were so many types of psychotherapy and to many individual differences in technique among therapists.

My own practice as a psychiatrist includes both psychotherapy and medication monitoring, and I do not think I am bragging when I say that the results I get when I combine medication with psychotherapy are better than those with medication monitoring alone. Studies have in fact been done comparing treatments for depression, and they show that the combination of medication and psychotherapy is more effective than either modality alone. Studies have also shown that when both modalities are done by a psychiatrist the overall treatment is more cost-effective than so-called combined therapy, in which the medications are monitored by a psychiatrist and the psychotherapy is delivered by a non-medical therapist (psychologist or social worker). The explanation for this is that although per-session reimbursements are higher for psychiatrists, they tend to require fewer sessions than non-medical psychotherapists in order to achieve the same patient outcomes.

One wonders whether clinical studies tend to investigate only psychotropic medications while excluding psychotherapy because the funding for them comes from pharmaceutical houses. It certainly did not escape my attention that funding for the studies presented at the symposium, as well as for the symposium itself, came from pharmaceutical companies.

The other phenomenon observable in psychiatry these days is the influence of HMOs, which encourage the use of medication by psychiatrists primarily through the procedure called 'medication monitoring,' which entails brief visits at intervals of a month or even more. The HMOs are under financial pressure to push for the psychotherapy to be handled by non-medical therapists, with psychiatrists doing only the brief medication monitoring visits. Psychiatrists, too, have a financial motivation to go along with this arrangement, since 15-minute medical monitoring visits are reimbursed at half the rate of a 45-minute psychotherapy session. For the doctor this means that a practice consisting entirely of brief visits is more lucrative than one involving combined treatment.

One gets the impression that a coalition of the pharmaceutical houses and the HMOs are now the ones determining how psychiatric treatment is delivered and by whom. This, in my opinion, is a very unfortunate situation. Owing to their more extensive training, psychiatrists are better qualified to make psychiatric evaluations, understand psychoses and understand the relationship between a patient's psychiatric problems and other medical conditions that may be present and which are themselves often related to emotional factors. In addition, good psychotherapy can produce effects and outcomes that no medication can duplicate. Perhaps it will take NIMH funding to widen the scope of clinical studies and find out which treatments for depressive and anxiety disorders are actually the most effective.

## TO THE EDITOR OF THE NEW YORK TIMES:

## Those Marvelous SSRIs, the Miracle Drugs of Psychiatry

In "FDA Links Drugs to Being Suicidal" we read about the controversy over the potential link between SSRI medications widely used in the treatment of psychiatric patients and suicide. Having been in psychiatry since the time when there were no medications at all for psychiatric disorders of any kind, I can say unequivocally that these medications are truly miracle drugs. Using them in conjunction with psychotherapy, I have been able to turn people's lives around, amazing even myself. I call them brain normalizers, because that is what they seem to be and that is how patients describe their experience taking them. Under no circumstances should media reports highlighting the risk of suicide scare people away from these medications. It is unfortunate but true that nearly all medications, including aspirin and penicillin, can provoke severe negative reactions in a small number of patients. It should in any case be obvious that before SSRIs are prescribed the patient in question needs to undergo a thorough examination by a psychiatrist. Once on the medication, the patient also needs to be carefully monitored on a weekly basis for at least 6 weeks until the medication's effects have stabilized. Primary care physicians and others not familiar with psychiatric disorders and the use of SSRIs should not be prescribing them.

## TO THE EDITOR OF THE NEW YORK TIMES:

### Those Marvelous Antidepressants

I strongly disagree with the opinions expressed in "The Depressing News About Antidepressants." I have been practicing psychiatry since a time when we had no psychotropic drugs of any kind, only electroconvulsive (shock) therapy which was used to treat major depressive disorders. (Despite popular misconceptions, it was highly effective, quite safe and had no placebo effect!) Then along came the first generation of antidepressants, the tricyclics Elavil, Tofranil, etc., which were also highly effective but had two major disadvantages: they had major side effects that precluded their use in many patients and were lethal in the event of an overdose. As the article points out, the latest generation of drugs, called SSRIs, are highly effective and their side effects are far less problematic (although there are nonetheless still some patients who cannot tolerate them). Their use has definitely increased the effectiveness of my clinical work. Studies have shown that a combination of psychotherapy and medication is better than either alone, and I personally also prefer the combined approach. I have quite literally turned people's lives around with these medications and have seen them bring about clinical improvements that I was never able to achieve with earlier drugs. I call these antidepressants 'brain normalizers' because many of my patients tell me they make them feel normal. The SSRIs are effective to various degrees in treating not only depressive disorders, but also a range of anxiety disorders.

Then there are those patients who are referred for medication by non-medical psychotherapists because they have not been satisfied with their clinical results and suspect a drug would be of help. I have seen definite clinical improvement following the introduction of medication in many such cases. I have observed that if either I or the patient discontinues the medication, there is often a recurrence of clinical symptoms, and when medication is resumed, the symptoms respond again. I doubt that this represents a placebo effect.

## TO THE EDITOR OF THE NEW YORK TIMES:

### Don't Be Afraid of SSRIs, Just Use Them Correctly!

"The Antidepressant Dilemma" is an important and timely contribution to the discussion on the safety of antidepressant medications known as SSRIs. As someone who has been practicing psychiatry since the days when we had no psychotropic medications of any value at all, I consider these newer 'brain normalizers' something like miracle drugs. They make it possible to literally turn people's lives around. It is true that they can be dangerously psycho-activating and can provoke suicidal impulses in certain cases. (A patient once said to me, "Don't give me Prozac—I took it once and I wanted to kill either myself or someone else!") The article correctly points out the main problem associated with their use, namely that there aren't enough child and adolescent psychiatrists with the proper training to administer them. This has resulted in patients being treated by pediatricians and family doctors who may not have training or experience in diagnosing and treating depression. Depression is often a serious illness which, if inadequately treated, can lead to suicidal behavior. No one would ask a psychiatrist, for instance, to prescribe antibiotics for medical conditions he or she is not trained or qualified to treat. In my opinion, pediatricians or family doctors who prescribe psychotropic medications should at the very least thoroughly educate themselves concerning proper diagnosis and follow-up treatment of depressive disorders, which includes monitoring such patients weekly for at least six weeks while paying special attention to possible side effects. Ideally they should develop a relationship with the patient, and if possible, schedule psychotherapy sessions to understand the patient better and look for signs of suicidal ideation. Prescribing medications and scheduling the first follow-up visit for a month later, as described in the article, is not good practice.

## TO THE EDITOR OF THE NEW YORK TIMES:

As a practicing psychiatrist I read with interest the discussion in the Science Times concerning the difficulty of proving the efficacy of psychotherapy. Since the early days of psychiatry when the only forms of treatment were electroconvulsive (shock) therapy and psychoanalysis, we have seen the emergence of a variety of psychotherapies and the development of two generations of psychotropic drugs, so that we now have a wide variety of modalities for the effective treatment of emotional disorders. Generally speaking, it is more difficult to evaluate the efficacy of psychotherapy in clinical trials than it is to evaluate the efficacy of drugs. However, there have been reliable clinical studies of treatments for depression in which psychotherapy alone, drugs alone and a combination of the two were given to a large number of patients. The combined treatment was shown to be more effective than either alone.

The new generation of drugs, the SSRIs and their cousins, are usually referred to as antidepressants, but I prefer to call them brain normalizers because they do just that. As much as these drugs help patients, psychotherapy is still an important part of treatment. It gives patients the support they need during the period of distress before the medication takes effect, it addresses the problems that caused the depression in the first place and it allows the psychotherapist to ensure that the patient is taken off the medication as soon as improvement sets in and circumstances allow. In addition, as alluded to in the article, a good match between patient and psychotherapist can bring about treatment outcomes which no medication can duplicate. The results that can be achieved using both modalities together are sometimes quite astounding, not only for depression, but even for a number of emotional disorders, though efficacy in the case of the latter can't be proven based on just a few cases. Extensive clinical studies are needed, and I predict they will prove that this approach is just as effective in treating other emotional disorders as it is for depression.

# Chapter 4

# RELIGION

RELIGION ATTRACTS THE INTEREST OF local and national politicians in America and influences their campaigns now perhaps more so than at any time in the past. Social and moral issues such as gay rights, gay marriage, the 'don't ask, don't tell' law, abortion and stem cell research have taken on increasing importance in elections and have been the focus of increasing attention in the media. Conservative views on all these questions have mostly paralleled conservative political identification and have sometimes had a crucial influence on choices in the voting booth nationwide.

This chapter includes, along with letters to editors, a number of letters to well-known religious figures in response to media coverage of their views. Among these are prominent evangelists who minister to enormous congregations and radio and television audiences numbering in the thousands and even millions: Dr. James Dobson of Focus on the Family, Pat Robertson of the 700 Club, Jerry Falwell of Liberty University, Billy Graham and his son Franklin, Joel Osteen in Texas, and Rev. Robert Schuller of the Crystal Cathedral in California. I have also included a letter I wrote to Harold Camping, a self-styled Bible expert and originator of the Open Forum, a call-in radio program in which Camping answers listeners' questions on biblical matters. These men all speak for the organizations they represent and express widely divergent theological opinions, many of which are controversial. What they have in common is that they have influenced public opinion, for better or worse. How they have amassed such followings and achieved such influence is in some cases a mystery. Other once-popular evangelists—Jimmy Swaggart, Ted Haggard and Jim Bakker, to name a few—have lost their following and departed from the scene in disgrace, in some cases to prison.

\* \* \*

## TO THE RELIGION EDITOR OF NEWSWEEK: OCTOBER, 2009

### Believers vs. Non-Believers

In "Two White Guys Walk into a Bar," Sylvia Miller discusses the recent increase in the publication of books questioning religious belief. According to her, the arguments presented in these books give voice to the 12 percent of Americans who say they don't believe in God, that is, the God of organized religion—the omnipotent, omniscient and omnipresent Father in Heaven in whom, according to Christians for instance, one must believe in order to have eternal life, etc.

Meanwhile, the mere convention of capitalizing the word God implicitly makes the statement that there is in fact such a god. Just because some people hold this belief, however, does not make it a fact. Believers take unfair semantic advantage by using language that presumes the existence of God as absolute fact. In reality, no one, not even the staunchest believer, knows that 'God' exists. If one wished to know a person's religious beliefs, instead of asking "Do you believe in God?" (i.e., the questioner's God) it would be more appropriate to ask "Do you think that in this universe there exists a god or not?"

A person who does not think that there is a god, but allows that there might be one, is not necessarily an atheist. One can reject organized religion with its tenets and beliefs and yet wonder what this world is all about, how it came to be and even whether there are forces working in it about which we know nothing.

Although 88% of Americans say they believe in God, I doubt that very many actually do. I say this because if people did, their behavior would be drastically different from what it is. Everyone would tithe at the very least, and churches would be rich from large donations. Such behaviors as crime, dishonesty, cheating, adultery, fornication and marital infidelity, to name just a few, would not occur at present levels if people really thought that an omniscient God was monitoring all their thoughts, wishes and behavior 24 hours a day. Ours would be a vastly different society altogether. Life would be full of morality, ethics, generosity, good will and all the other virtues that are so lacking nowadays. In my opinion, people who profess to believe in God do so only because they fear that they will be ostracized in this life and possibly punished in an afterlife. In essence, they're afraid to admit that they don't believe what they've been taught—in case it turns out to be true!

## TO THE EDITOR OF THE NEW YORK TIMES: NOVEMBER 2010

## Atheists and Believers

The Pew Research Center conducted a survey recently of atheists, Catholics, Protestants and Jews concerning knowledge about religion. The results showed that the atheists knew considerably more about religion than the believers. This is not surprising, as most atheists are former believers who studied and thought about the subject and decided that what believers are told to believe is not believable.

For instance, the report says that many Catholics do not understand Communion, the doctrine of transubstantiation according to which the Communion wine literally becomes the blood of Jesus. And who can blame them? I doubt in a medical emergency anyone would want to receive a transfusion of Communion wine.

As for the grossly subjective morality of most televangelists who claim that homosexuality goes against the Bible and is therefore sinful, I would point out that Jesus himself said nothing on the subject. The passage most frequently quoted in this connection is from the Old Testament Book of Leviticus, in which homosexuality is called an "abomination"—along with eating shrimp and seeing your father naked!

On the other hand, Jesus said plenty about adultery; namely, that anyone who marries a divorced person is committing adultery (thus violating one of the Ten Commandments). Saint Paul, meanwhile, described all sexual behavior out of wedlock as fornication and told unmarried women and widows that therefore "it is better to marry than to burn."

I have a feeling that if our most popular church leaders emphasized these sins in their sermons, their large followings would quickly dwindle and churches everywhere would have an awful lot of empty pews. Atheists are scorned because they know more about what religions actually teach and this is threatening to believers, who are unsure of their beliefs but afraid to face their doubts.

As Martin Luther said, "reason is enemy of religion."

## TO THE EDITOR OF NEWSWEEK:

## The Curiousness of Christian Beliefs

I found "The Birth of Jesus" (Newsweek, December 13, 2004, p. 49) as intriguing as it was comprehensive. In it, the author lays out the many inconsistencies and contradictions in Christian theology and belief. The words that leapt off the page were those of

Rev. H. B. London Jr., vice-president of Focus on the Family, who was quoted as saying, "I don't want to be too simplistic, but our faith is somewhat childlike. Though other people may question the historical validity of the virgin birth, and the death and resurrection of Jesus Christ, we don't."

What a naive confession by someone who has suspended rational thinking in the service of his need to believe in the all-knowing, benevolent and protecting father in heaven! (Has anyone ever stopped to consider that if Jesus had actually bodily risen and ascended even ten miles towards heaven, he would have frozen to death?) Its childlike simplicity is such that one could almost make an analogy with the belief in Santa Claus. And this is the problem with religious beliefs: wherever there is such an overriding need for reassurance about what happens after death (which, I'll admit, is kind of scary), rationality has to be ignored because reality is too frightening. Meanwhile, no one knows what actually happens after death—not even the Pope—and none of us can know until it happens to us. Maturity requires that this fact be faced. The only consolation is that we are all in the same boat and there's nothing we can do about it. If there is an afterlife, we'll all participate equally (thank God!).

## TO THE EDITOR OF THE NEW YORK TIMES:

## God-Believers

What puzzles me about god-believers (people who claim they believe in a god) is that for centuries they have been killing each other in great numbers in the name of their gods. From the Crusades and the Spanish Inquisition right up to the current 'troubles' in Ireland and the warring between Israel and the Palestinians.

Let's face it: if there is a personal god responsible for this world, there is only one of him (or her, or it). It obviously follows from this that all other specific belief systems—all the other people who are convinced that theirs is the only true religion and everybody else is an infidel or heathen—are wrong. Atheists, too, have traditionally come in for special contempt and loathing in some religions, sometimes to the extent that their murder has been condoned or even perpetrated by god-believers. Basically, god-believers have displayed their intolerance of others at all times and places. I can only think that the one true god, if there is one, must be mortified, to put it mildly, by the bitter animosities and hatred, the violence and outright carnage that is perpetrated in that god's name.

Interestingly, I have never heard of an atheist who killed anyone over religious belief. The key seems to be that, as the famous theologian Reinhold Niebuhr said, "religious fanaticism is based on doubt." That is, god-believers cannot tolerate dissent in any form because it poses too great a threat to their own shaky belief system. The religious are highly motivated to be intolerant, and they're good at it.

And what do we make of Jerry Falwell's claim that his God used Islamic terrorists to kill innocent Americans in the World Trade Center as a way to punish our country for being tolerant of gays, lesbians and pro-choice advocates? How could a mass murder with that motive conceivably be attributed to the benevolent, loving and just God people like Falwell otherwise claim him to be? (The answer, of course, is that it can't. The reality is that Jerry Falwell himself has a profound hatred of Americans. Tellingly, he apologized for the "insensitivity and timing" of his statement, but not for the vicious, immoral views he had expressed.)

It would make far more sense for god-believers to unite in their relationship to the one god of this world, if he/she/it exists, instead of fighting with each other over relatively minor differences in their beliefs in an attempt to make or prove themselves the favored followers. I frankly can't imagine a god who would be indifferent to hatred, fighting and murder perpetrated in his/her/its name.

While many Americans right now are praying to their God during this sad and frightening time, Reverends Falwell and Robertson are convinced that their God is using Islamic terrorists to punish this country for having what they consider to be immoral attitudes. While we all look for reassurance to calm our fears, these 'men of God' are doing their best to intensify them. With their inflammatory comments they are making an already stressful situation worse, and are, in fact, assisting the terrorists by further traumatizing our nation. In other words, they themselves are the religious terrorists, and always have been. If the God they worship is as they say He is, they can have Him.

Sometimes I just thank the gods I'm an atheist.


## TO THE EDITOR OF BUSINESS WEEK: NOVEMBER 26, 2004


## The Age of Hypo-Christianity

There has been a lot in the press lately about proposals for laws to deal with the increasing visibility of homosexuals in America, including laws on sodomy, laws to ban gay marriage, laws strengthening gay rights, laws concerning gays in the military, etc. Religious groups have also been actively making their views known, especially conservative Christian groups who cite scripture to argue that homosexuality is immoral and sinful. The Episcopal Church is on the verge of a major split over the issue of consecrating overtly gay bishops. Groups promoting family values claim that homosexuality is a threat to the family and cite the Bible, chiefly the Old Testament Book of Leviticus, and the Judeo-Christian tradition in general.

It would make sense, then, to actually look in the Bible and see what it says about homosexuality and heterosexuality, and then decide whether there is a need for legislation regulating the rights of non-heterosexual members of society.

The first interesting thing we notice is that Jesus himself apparently said almost nothing about sexuality per se. He did, however, have some very definite things to say about marriage and divorce. He said that "if a man puts his wife out in divorce, except for fornication, he makes her an adulteress, and if a man marries a divorced woman, he is committing adultery."

Now, adultery is a serious matter—remember the Ten Commandments? Based on the teachings of Christ as set down in the Bible, one would expect Christians to stand for strict laws forbidding divorce and remarriage, perhaps even a Constitutional amendment! As recently as the 1940s when I was in my early training to be a psychiatrist, the only grounds for divorce recognized in New York State were five years of incurable insanity in a spouse. Today, divorce has become so prevalent in the U.S. that a minority of households are headed by married couples.

What about fornication, which according to Saint Paul includes *any* sexual relations outside of marriage by anyone anywhere? Based on this, wouldn't one expect Christians to support laws banning any and all non-marital sexual activity? Or have they perhaps somehow inadvertently overlooked these direct biblical pronouncements on marriage and sexuality?

Alas, in these cases and others, it is clear to see that scripture is cited selectively by various religious and political groups to rationalize their own agendas and impose their own particular idea of morality on the rest of society.

## TO THE EDITOR OF THE NEW YORK TIMES:

## Belief vs. Science

In "A Call to Catholics to Trust What Cannot Be Seen" (April 20, 2010, p. A22), we read that in a homily delivered at St. Patrick's Cathedral the newly installed Archbishop of New York, Timothy Michael Dolan, called on his flock to build their faith on "trust in what cannot be seen" and not only "on empirical, scientific evidence." His comments echo Martin Luther's assertion centuries ago that "reason is the enemy of religion." How true! Bishop Dolan is telling us, in effect, to eschew what is known to be true through the study of concrete evidence—in other words, reality—and put our faith in what we hope is true but will not know to be true until we die. In other words, let your beliefs, not facts, be your reality. What century is the Bishop living in?

## Do They Really Believe in God?

The recently televised debates among the 2008 presidential candidates included questions about their religious beliefs. Nearly all of them stated explicitly that they believe in God and that religion is an important part of their lives. Some even confessed that Jesus was their savior. Only Senator Hilary Clinton commented that she was suspect of those who "wear their religion on their sleeves," which many certainly seemed to be doing that evening. Polls report that upwards of 95% of Americans say that they believe in God. Just as it would be political suicide for a politician to admit not believing in God, the majority of the population are afraid to admit to being non-believers lest they be branded atheists, who are still pariahs in our society.

The practice of silent prayer assumes that human thoughts become known directly to the God-intelligence, whatever and wherever it may be. If this is the case, there must be something like a miniature radio station in each human being transmitting all of his or her thoughts, ideas and impulses through the atmosphere directly to this God, and He/She/It must be constantly monitoring the entirety of all human mental activity.

Imagine, though, how different human behavior and human society would be if people actually believed that this God was privy to their every thought and impulse. It seems to me that things would be very different, indeed. Churches would be filled to capacity; in fact, many more would have to be built! The milk of human kindness would flow endlessly and the spirit of Christmas would be felt all year round. Adults would behave like model children in a school with strict discipline. Things would really be different!

I suspect there would also be long waiting lines outside of confessional booths and equally long waiting lists for appointments with psychiatrists. People would be terrified by the awareness that their evil thoughts and impulses were being broadcast to this God-intelligence and by the prospect of being punished by Him.

As it is, many people can barely cope with the fact that they have thoughts and impulses that their conscience doesn't allow them to accept in themselves.

## TO THE EDITOR OF THE RECORD:

## Atheism is Not a Religion

The 2008 presidential candidates are on the spot to confess their religious beliefs as in no previous election. It is said that an atheist could never be elected to the White House and that it would be political suicide for a candidate not to be affiliated with a religious faith.

Of course, we know that claiming to believe in God and actually believing in God are two different things. If everyone who said they believed in the God if Christianity really did, ours would be a different society altogether. America is hardly a Christian country, despite what some presidential candidates have asserted. If you go by the Bible, America is actually a land of adulterers and fornicators, since the New Testament teaches Christians that *all* remarried divorcees are adulterers and *all* sex outside of marriage is fornication.

Atheists in America are seen as pariahs, an evil bunch of dissidents and a threat to religion and society. Only last week the Pope advised Catholics not to see a certain movie that he felt encouraged atheism. In fact, however, atheism is neither a cult nor a movement aimed at debunking any religion. Atheists do not preach and do not attempt to convert others to their beliefs. They do not view Christians with hatred and intolerance, as Christians do atheists.

A term which more accurately describes the views of people known as atheists is non-believer. Non-believers are not against any belief system, they simply don't subscribe to one. After all, no one, including the Pope in Rome, knows for certain that there is a living

Father-God in the sky who is omniscient, omnipotent, omnipresent, etc. The existence of a god is the premise of religious belief systems, not a fact. The question "Do you believe in God?" should really be preceded by the question "Do you believe in the existence of a deity?" The non-believer's answer would be simply "No, I don't."

This is why non-believers are not threatened by those who disagree with them in the way that many people with strong religious beliefs are. Those among the latter who condemn non-believers to hell or wish death upon infidels merely reveal that they have doubts and unconsciously fear that the slightest test might undermine their positions. As Reinhold Niebuhr one said, "religious fanaticism is rooted in doubt." Christians used to execute heretics and some Muslims still do. Do they really think their God approves of this?

When you come right down to it, the minority of non-believers have as much chance of being right as believers, because either there is or there isn't a supreme God as described by the various religions. Just because the vast majority of Americans say they believe in God doesn't make their position more likely to be true than the position of the minority who don't believe.

## Some Thoughts on the Easter Story

The Easter story exemplifies our society's failure to reconcile science and religion, and this inconsistency may account for some of the widespread disaffection of our children. Children (and adults) in this country are exposed to so much mutually contradictory information and so many irrational ideas that it is difficult for them to trust those who promulgate such misinformation.

A former Roman Catholic Bishop, speaking about Easter and the idea that Jesus actually rose bodily off the Earth, recently posed the question "What do you suppose an astrophysicist would say to that?" The image of the resurrection and bodily ascension into heaven only makes sense if one still believes that the world is flat, as people did 2000 years ago. Ascension up into heaven would not be 'up' nowadays, but 'out'—that is, into space—and the precise direction would depend on the destination and the time of day when this ascension took place. As for the heaven to which Jesus is alleged to have ascended, any physical location in the three-dimensional universe where living beings could conceivably exist would have to be light years away. So if Jesus did in fact bodily ascend to that alleged place, he would still be on his way and would be visible through the Hubble telescope!

Religious zealots in the Bible belt are trying to resolve these inconsistencies by introducing the biblical version of creation into the school curriculum in order to legitimize their primitive religious beliefs and prevent any reality-based challenges to them. How can our young people believe in anything these days when they are expected to believe in such irrational ideas promulgated by their elders at home and in the church? They know that such nonsensical assertions fly in the face of reality and are no more rational than was the prevailing belief when the Bible was written that the world is flat.

Why can't our leaders be honest so that young people can believe in them?

## TO THE EDITOR OF THE NEW YORK TIMES: FEBRUARY, 2002

## God at the Super Bowl

This week I heard two of the silliest remarks ever about the workings of a deity. One was by a man who works in the dump on Staten Island where the debris from the WTC attack ends up. His unpleasant job is to recover body parts and personal effects of victims of the attack. His remark was that God was surely there at work helping him to find what he was looking for. Well, if you ask me that help came a bit late in the day! Where was God on September 11th?

The answer, according to Jerry Falwell and Pat Robertson, is that God was there on 9/11, sure enough, but He let the attack happen as a way to punish America for tolerating gays, lesbians and abortionists. As I understand it, the God that people say they believe in could certainly have stopped that event, if he had wanted to, so therefore either he didn't care (as Jackie Onassis said in her later years, "if there is a God, he is cruel") or he was asleep. Billy Graham, speaking at the WTC memorial service at Washington Cathedral, confessed that over the years he had often been asked why God let things like this happen but that he had never come to a satisfactory answer.

The other absurd remark about a deity was one made by the owner of the New England Patriots when he attributed the team's victory in Super Bowl XXXVI to "the work of God."

In other words, we are to believe that this God was asleep on September 11th, woke up in time to help recover body parts at the dump, and then stopped off in New Orleans to see to it that the Patriots won! With all the conflict, misery and suffering going on all over the world, God is working on winning a football game in New Orleans. (Can you imagine Jesus at a football game?)

As theologians have often said, God works in mysterious ways. So it seems!

## TO THE EDITOR OF THE NEW YORK TIMES:

## Pat Roberston, Billy Graham and God

Pat Robertson now reports (The New York Times, May 19, 2006) that God told him personally that a tsunami would hit America this summer and that Ariel Sharon's stroke was punishment for his having withdrawn from Gaza. This is just the latest ranting of this unbelievable man.

Billy Graham, meanwhile, recently asserted that God created not only this world, but all the other planets, stars and galaxies as well. Last year he said that he had seen heaven and "it was beautiful, like a family reunion." He also claimed that Natalie Holloway's disappearance in Aruba and the death of three children in an automobile trunk in Camden, N.J., were signs that the end was near. "I believe that God is warning us," he said.

To threaten an already anxious nation is hardly a message of hope. To intimate that God uses such tragedies to warn people that they must repent in order to be saved is beyond belief. And to cite these two isolated pieces of news as evidence that the end times are near is downright bizarre. Perhaps Graham has been listening to that other laughable prophet, Harold Camping of the Open Forum, who predicted that on April 21, 2011, we would see the end of the world, which he calls the Rapture. (On April 22, the day after the Rapture didn't come to pass, he said he was "flabbergasted." I guess Mr. Camping flabbergasts easily. He then advanced the date to October 21, 2011.)

These three men of God appear to have severed their ties with reality and are either experiencing hallucinations and delusions or are downright prevaricators. However laughable their pronouncements, they cannot technically be called psychotic, since irrational beliefs are not considered pathological if they are accepted by a significant portion of society.

## TO THE EDITOR OF THE NEW YORK TIMES: NOVEMBER 5, 2010

### Pat Robertson, Our First Christian Terrorist

Pat Robertson, the so-called Christian clergyman, is on record as having asserted that the catastrophic earthquake in Haiti was caused by Satan in retribution for the Haitians' having broken a pact with him in the past, or some such nonsense. Robertson had previously stated that God "let 9/11 happen" to punish America for its tolerant attitude towards gays and abortion.

The man certainly has an active imagination, but he is also clearly preoccupied with cruelty, destruction, death and terror. His image of God is not a very reassuring one and it certainly bears no resemblance to the loving God of Christianity, for instance. Robertson's intent, it seems clear, is simply to sow as much fear as possible—that being the basic goal of any terrorist. Years ago, Reinhold Niebuhr, the noted theologian, remarked that there is no more dangerous person than one who claims to know what God thinks. Fortunately, Pat Robertson is so off-the-wall that no one takes him seriously, so in that sense I guess he's just an amateur, not a real terrorist. He also isn't a real Christian, as far as I can tell. If I had to choose one word to describe him, I'd just say he's nuts.

## SEPTEMBER 2008

### Pat Robertson in Lipstick

We all heard the question asked recently by Governor Sarah Palin "What's the difference between a hockey mom and a pit bull?—Answer: Lipstick." Well, my question is What's the difference between Sarah Palin and Pat Robertson?—Answer: Lipstick. Pat Robertson tells us that God allowed 9/11 to happen, and Sarah Palin tells us that the war in Iraq is God's plan. In the words of the distinguished theologian Reinhold Niebuhr, "There is no more dangerous person than one who claims to know what God is thinking."

Jerry Falwell, President
Liberty University
1972 University Blvd
Lynchburg, VA 24502-2269

Dear Rev. Falwell:

Having just seen you make a fool of yourself on Crossfire (April 25, 2001), I thought I'd write and point out a few gross instances in which you revealed yourself during that program to be misinformed and ignorant.

In the first place, your calling Dr. Elders "nuts" was completely out of place, rude and inexcusable. That she didn't rebuke you on the spot shows what a lady she is. Contrary to your assertions, her comments about masturbation are entirely accurate. Most youngsters masturbate. In fact, any teenager who hasn't is probably suffering from severe emotional inhibition and needs psychological help. It is a normal, harmless part of adolescence. The only harm comes from the guilt some youngsters develop as a result of listening to the moralizing disapproval of ignorant people like yourself.

Many people cite the story of Onan, who "spilt his seed on the ground," as proof that the Bible condemns masturbation. In fact, this story has nothing to do with masturbation. Onan was confronted with the Old Testament rule that the surviving brother should satisfy his deceased brother's widow sexually, and he refused to do it. Did Jesus ever say anything about masturbation? As far as I am aware, and as far as I can recall from Sunday school, Jesus' messages to his followers included very little, if anything, about sexuality. If you can cite anything in the Bible on masturbation, New or Old Testament, I would like to hear about it.

As for extramarital sex in our society, it is a fact of life and anyone who points out that you are trying to foist your particular sexual morals on the whole country is absolutely correct. Most people, even quite religious people in some denominations, do not consider extramarital sex sinful or immoral. As a matter of fact, did Jesus ever say anything about any sort of sexual behavior, extramarital or otherwise? If so, I would appreciate your quoting chapter and verse for me.

Certainly Saint Paul had things to say about sexual behavior. In my opinion, however, his views on the subject are extreme, unhealthy and abnormal (Some theologians believe Paul was gay. What do you think?) In his first letter to the Corinthians he admonished everyone to be "as I am," by which he presumably meant celibate. Is this healthy or even desirable? Elsewhere the Bible says "be fruitful and multiply."

Paul remarks that in order not to fornicate, one should marry, for "it is better to marry than to burn." Is this a healthy attitude towards love and marriage—marry so you won't fornicate? He never mentioned that one should marry for love and have children. Paul, we see, was himself sexually inhibited and had a strange view indeed of love and marriage.

As for homosexuality, the comments you made reveal your abysmal ignorance of human psychosexual development and prevailing medical views on the origins of homosexuality. When the Bible is quoted on this subject it is usually from the book of Leviticus, where we read that "for mankind to sleep with mankind as with womankind is an abomination." I suppose it is possible that back then they noticed that homosexuality increased the risk of the spread of sexually transmitted diseases. Oddly, though, as I am sure you are aware, the same passage also calls it an "abomination" for a man to *see his father or uncle naked or to eat shellfish.*

You have expressed the opinion that people choose their sexual orientation, but by saying this you merely reveal your complete ignorance. When I was just starting out in psychiatric practice many homosexuals spent a lot time and money on psychiatric treatment in an attempt to be 'cured' of this unwanted condition and change their sexual orientation. However, this is very difficult to accomplish, if not impossible, even when the patient and psychiatrist both try their best. We now know that the difficulty stems from the fact that sexual orientation is determined very early in life, long before a person is capable of making a conscious choice in the matter. Furthermore, even if it were possible, the notion that anyone would consciously choose to be homosexual in the face of such societal condemnation of the lifestyle is patently ridiculous.

No one really knows the whole story of what causes homosexuality. Most likely it involves a genetic predisposition combined with poor gender identification, possibly as a consequence of family dynamics. In some cases, it has been traced to a fear of heterosexuality in childhood related to overattachment to the mother and poor identification with the father. However, it is always a matter of multiple causality.

Eventually, the American Psychiatric Association came to the view that homosexuality is not a disease but merely a variation on normal development. This relieved a lot of the intense guilt and self-loathing that in the past had frequently led to suicide among young homosexuals. Condemnation of homosexual behavior by the Catholic Church and others also used to contribute to that unfortunate state of affairs. Inasmuch as society has now become more tolerant of homosexuality, I rarely hear of patients any more who are interested in changing their sexual orientation or who commit suicide out of guilt over it, although it does still happen occasionally.

Wake up, Reverend Falwell, and learn something about human sexuality so you can be informed and talk sensibly on the subject and not make such a fool of yourself on national television!

## TO THE EDITOR OF THE NEW YORK TIMES:

## Reverend Falwell's Heavenly Timing

In "Reverend Falwell's Heavenly Timing" (May 20, 2007, Section 4, p. 13) Frank Rich says much of what needs to said about the legacy of Rev. Jerry Falwell. He and his buddy Pat Robertson are of like minds, as Robertson not only agreed with Falwell's assertion that God let 9/11 happen as punishment for America's attitude toward abortion and gays, but he also recently claimed that God told him, Pat Robertson, that there would be a major terrorist attack in America in 2007 involving thousands of victims. More guys who think they know what God is thinking!

## TO THE EDITOR OF THE NEW YORK TIMES:

## The Rev. Franklin Graham's Misinformation

In her August 22, 2010, column Maureen Dowd quotes the Rev. Franklin Graham as stating "I think the president's problem is that he was born a Muslim. His father was a Muslim. The seed of Islam is passed through the father like the seed of Judaism is passed through the mother." Graham should know, of course, that Jewishness is a nationality, specifically of those descended from the early Hebrew tribes, and Judaism is their religion. Islam, meanwhile, is a religion, not a nationality. Followers of Islam, called Muslims, are found among many nationalities: Iranians, Iraqis, Malaysians, etc. There is no Islamic seed.

At a more basic level, no one is truly born into a religion, since religion is based on the acceptance of a specific set of beliefs, and no newborn can believe in anything. So, for example, being baptized as a baby doesn't make one a Christian; one becomes a Christian when one espouses Christian beliefs and practices. The same is true for Muslims and Islam. Even Reverend Graham was not born a Christian; he was born into a Christian family.

Oddly, for someone who calls himself a Christian he does seem awfully interested in stirring up yet more trouble between Christians and Muslims—as if the trouble we hear about through the media all day long weren't enough. (When the United States invaded Iraq, he wanted to go there and convert the Muslims to Christianity—certainly one of the dumbest contributions to the war effort ever proposed!) He was up to more troublemaking when he made his ignorant and misleading remark that President Obama was born a Muslim, knowing it would fan the flames of political acrimony toward the president in today's already overheated atmosphere.

## TO THE EDITOR OF THE RECORD:

## Church Denies Wheat-Free Communion

In "Church Denies Wheat-Free Communion" we read of a Catholic church's refusal to grant a young boy's request on dietary grounds for a wheat-free Communion wafer. A policy less Christian than this one—coming from a Christian Church!—I cannot possibly imagine. Apparently Catholic clergy either don't read the Bible any more or else don't place much stock in what Jesus himself had to say. One of the first Bible verses taught in any Sunday School is "Suffer the little children to come unto me and forbid them not, for of such is the Kingdom of God." That church in Monmouth County is telling that boy to get lost—literally, figuratively and spiritually. Would Jesus invalidate the boy's Communion?

## TO THE EDITOR OF THE NEW YORK TIMES:

## Not-So-Intelligent Design

In "Sleepy Election Is Jolted by Evolution" the term 'intelligent design'—conservative Christians' thinly disguised term for creationism—appears again, referring to the idea that the world and all that is in it was created by the God of Christianity. The article discusses efforts to teach intelligent design as an alternative to evolution in high schools and asserts that "across the country, more and more school districts are coming to grips with the idea that intelligent design is a theory that should be taught alongside evolution."

I, for one, would like to question the level of intelligence involved in designing a world which includes underwater earthquakes that cause tsunamis, volcanoes, hurricanes, tornadoes and other devastating natural phenomena. And what sort of intelligence would seriously consider creating the viruses we call Ebola, polio (something just for kids!) and HIV? The latter has afflicted over 25 million Africans and has orphaned many thousands if not millions. What about deadly microbes such as malaria, tuberculosis, syphilis, influenza and leprosy? What about man-eating sharks, venomous snakes and poisonous plants? What about human beings, who are capable of massacring each other and spend a lot of their time doing it? This list of horrors could only have been designed by an intelligence with a deeply ambivalent attitude toward mankind.

## TO THE EDITOR OF THE NEW YORK TIMES:

### Missionaries in Iraq—A Real Bad Idea

In "Top Evangelicals Critical of Colleagues Over Islam" it was reported that, while evangelical leaders denounced anti-Islam remarks made by leaders of their own movement as "dangerous" and "unhelpful" and proposed new guidelines for churches to follow in relating to Muslims, they also "reaffirmed their commitment to proselytizing" and were "deeply divided over whether their goal should be to coexist with Muslims or to convert them." (As if they could.)

Of all the bad ideas that have been proposed to help this country's efforts to democratize Iraq this by far has to be the worst and most dangerous! The mere voicing of these views by a few religious leaders will go a long way toward confirming Muslims' suspicions that the United States government has ulterior motives in its 'liberation' of Iraq, namely, to establish a Christian state there. Can you imagine the reaction in America if Islamic clerics in Iraq were to announce that they had set themselves the goal of eventually converting American Christians to Islam?

It would appear that there are radical Christians who are no more interested in coexisting with other religions than some radical Muslims.

# TO THE EDITOR OF THE NEW YORK POST:

## Two Humdingers

Two recent articles in the September 10, 2001, edition of the Post offered extraordinary glimpses into Christianity in action. In one, it was reported that Mother Teresa had suffered from insomnia in the last days of her life in the hospital and that the Archbishop of Calcutta, believing her sleeplessness to be cause by an evil spirit, had called in a priest to exorcise it.

In the other, Reverend Adrian Condit, the father of Senator Gary Condit, went on record saying that he thought Chandra Levy's disappearance in Washington, D.C., and probable death had been the work of Satan.

In other words, here are two reports indicating that the thinking of some Christian clergy active today is still in the Middle Ages, at best.

# TO THE EDITOR OF THE NEW YORK TIMES:

## Christian Believers, So They Say

A recent article in the Times told the unfortunate story of the imminent bankruptcy of the Crystal Cathedral of California, for many decades the pulpit of its founder, the Rev. Robert Schuller, in the face of insurmountable debts totaling $45,000,000. Rev. Schuller's radio broadcasts once had millions of followers. It was reported that many have now shifted their attention to Rev. Osteen, the Texan evangelist who preaches that anyone can attain riches if they listen to him and 'believe.' Accordingly, financial support for Rev. Schuller has diminished dramatically.

Not only is Schuller's church going bankrupt, so is the religion of its followers. It seems clear to me that if Schuller's millions of followers really believed in a God who was watching them 24 hours a day and all that goes with such a belief, they would happily make the sacrifice and wipe out the church's debt in a hurry—for God's sake! It would be the least they could do in gratitude for His emotional support and comfort over the years.

Of course, many people feel compelled to go to church and declare their belief in God simply because no to do so would cause them to be reviled by those around them whose faith is similarly shaky. In our current cultural atmosphere, not to profess one's faith is tantamount to inviting ostracism, as we saw during the last presidential campaign. All the candidates made a point of proclaiming their faith—because nowadays let's face it, if they didn't, they could never be elected to the White House (even though Thomas Jefferson was a self-proclaimed atheist).

## TO THE EDITOR OF THE NEW YORK TIMES:

### Apologies Are Due Michael Schiavo

In "Schiavo Autopsy Says Brain, Withered, Was Untreatable" (June 16, 2005, p. A1) the Times reported that Terri Schiavo's brain was severely damaged—it weighed only half its normal weight—and that she was, in fact, brain-dead. She was also blind and showed no signs of consciousness. Taken together, this meant that there was absolutely no hope of improvement in her medical condition. Such were the medical facts behind the clinical outcome in her case—or, put in religious terms, such was God's will.

The time has now come for all those who criticized Terri Schiavo's husband Michael and tried to thwart his wish to have Terri's feeding tube disconnected to apologize for causing him such pain and distress. The following is a list of those who should apologize to Mr. Schiavo: President Bush, for calling a special session of Congress to discuss the matter and possibly act on it; members of Congress, especially Senator Bill Frist for his inept neurological guesswork (he should know better), and Representative Tom DeLay, who voted in favor of the bill to allow the Florida State Court to consider the case; Reverend Jerry Falwell (who is wrong about most things); Reverend Jesse Jackson (for grandstanding); all those Christian evangelists and conservatives who acted in such an unchristian way and fought to keep the feeding tube in place; and anyone else who publicly criticized, threatened or attacked the character of Mr. Schiavo for his position in this intensely personal matter.

We now know that Mr. Schiavo, and the examining neurologists who after very careful study of his wife's condition pronounced her to be in a permanent vegetative state, were right. All his critics were wrong—and, more to the point, it was never any of their business in the first place.

## TO THE EDITOR OF THE NEW YORK TIMES:

Thomas Friedman's op-ed piece (November 26, 2001) entitled "The Real War" touches on a curious issue which traditional religious leaders, especially the more fanatical ones, have assiduously avoided. As the eminent theologian Reinhold Niebuhr once said, "religious fanaticism is rooted in doubt."

The issue, in a nutshell, is this: if there is a God who created the world and all living things in it, there can only be one of Him/She/It. (Does this God have a gender?) What, then, do theologians imagine this one God thinks (assuming He/She/It thinks as we humans do) of the long history of intolerance, hostility, killing, holy wars, jihads, crusades, inquisitions and child-killing (as in Northern Ireland ) perpetrated in His/Her/Its name by adherents of religions claiming Him/She/It for their own?

It has been reported recently that the Pope has "apologized" for the "misdeeds" committed over the centuries by the Catholic Church he heads. (Given that 'misdeeds' is a understatement of historic proportions, the idea that a mere "apology" could possibly be adequate is obscene.)

And as for Reverend Jerry Falwell—that self-appointed leader of the Taliban for Christ—if the God he worships really did use Islamic terrorists to punish America by attacking the World Trade Center, as he asserts He did, he can have his God and his horrifying theology. If Falwell is considered a good Christian, I thank God I'm an atheist!

The vast majority of the self-styled religious people of this world should be deeply ashamed of themselves for their arrogant narcissism, bigoted intolerance and self-righteous cruelty toward members of other faiths and to people generally. Of course they reserve their highest levels of hostility for those who do not believe in God at all, i.e., atheists, or, as the Muslims call them, infidels. The mere existence of non-believers awakens self-doubt in all but the most committed believers and are therefore a threat and cannot be tolerated. Curiously, I have never heard of atheists killing or waging wars in defense of their beliefs; in fact, as a rule they are tolerant of all religions and have no interest in converting anyone.

If the religious people of this world really believe what they claim, I suggest they get together as fast as possible and start acting like the children of God they profess to be, since I imagine He/She/It is not very pleased with what they have done in His/Her/Its name so far.

## TO THE EDITOR OF THE NEW YORK TIMES:

## An Accusation of Heresy—The Dark Ages Revisited

In "Seeing Heresy in a Service for Sept. 11" (February 8, 2002, p. B1) it was reported that Rev. David Benke is being accused of heresy for attempting to bring together and showing tolerance toward other religions of the world. How ironic that the Lutherans of the Missouri Synod are still trying to assert their ecumenical exclusiveness and superiority at a time when just such intolerances are threatening to destroy our very existence. They even speak of punishment for Benke. Since we seem to be back in the Middle Ages, religiously speaking, I wonder what form they will suggest this punishment take—burning at the stake?

They seem utterly unaware that hatred and intolerance has been the cause of killing and wars throughout history and continues even today within Christianity, with the "Troubles" in Northern Ireland between Catholics and Protestants.

The most pathetic statement of all was the one made by Rev. Steven Bohler, who said "It gives the appearance that their God and our God are the same, and they are not, or there are valid other religions, and there are none." If indeed there is a God who is responsible for starting and monitoring this world, there must obviously be only one, and each of the religions seems to be fighting for His exclusive approval, just like children. If indeed this God exists and 'thinks' in our sense of the word, I wonder what He thinks of all the dissention, hatred, and carnage that is perpetrated in His name?

The Lutheran Missouri Synod has always been a few hundred years behind the times. As far as I know they are still against cremation of the dead on the grounds that it might interfere with the resurrection of the body!

## TO THE EDITOR OF THE NEW YORK TIMES:

Bill Keller's brilliant and informative op-ed piece (May 4, 2002) pretty much says it all about the Catholic Church's real problem, and in my opinion a second major Christian Reformation is at hand. Only this time it won't be initiated by a lone monk, but by a groundswell of enlightened members of the church—nuns, liberal clergy and informed parishioners—who are fed up with leaders who in so many cases still haven't acknowledged the truth of what everyone else knows about the universe, the planet, human psychology and sexuality, epidemiology and the realities of modern life in the Western world. The Apostles' Creed, the summation of Christian belief repeated weekly in most Christian churches, still assumes that the world is flat. It states, "He descended into hell; the third day He rose again from the dead. He ascended into heaven . . ." Do they still really believe that hell is down, as in toward the center of the Earth? or that there is only one direction called 'up'? What was once thought of as 'up' we now know to be 'out' into outer space. The nearest destination where there could possibly be a physical heaven is beyond the known planets, light years away.

# TO THE EDITOR OF THE NEW YORK TIMES: NOVEMBER 2010

## Interest in Exorcism is Revived

My first reaction after reading "For Catholics, Interest in Exorcism is Revived" was to burst out laughing. My next reaction was to write this letter and state unequivocally that anyone who is convinced, or is even open to the suggestion by others, that they are possessed by the devil is delusional and is suffering from a major psychosis. A delusion is defined in psychiatry as a false belief that can't be shaken by reason. From what I gather, before an exorcism is attempted the procedure is to have a psychiatrist examine the allegedly possessed individual in order to determine whether that individual is delusional or actually possessed by the devil. One would have to question the competence of any psychiatrist who claimed to be able to make such a determination. (I doubt any legitimate psychiatrist would actually agree to offer an opinion on the matter.) This is yet another instance in which Catholic clergy reveal their remarkable ignorance of human psychology. I am reminded of a comment made by the then Bishop of Palm Beach, who had been accused of having sexually molested a child 25 years earlier and said "Twenty-five years ago we didn't even know it was a condition. We just thought, 'make a good confession and sin no more.'" Apparently back then he and his colleagues really did think that pedophilia was nothing out of the ordinary! Now they want to normalize delusional psychoses. Sadly, the Catholic Church's concept of mental health still seems to be firmly rooted in medieval superstition.

## TO THE EDITOR OF THE NEW YORK TIMES:

## Prayer at Football Games

A front page article in the New York Times on August 27, 2000, reported on the controversy over saying the Lord's Prayer at high school football games in the South. Praying to God and Jesus at football games is incomprehensible to me. What is the content of the petition? Is it to win the game and maim as many of the other team's players as possible—the ostensible aim of any game of football? Is it to protect the home team from injuries? In any case, invoking God at an activity that is the epitome of violence and mayhem—essentially a ritualized battle between communities—has precious little to do with Christianity and Jesus Christ. Could you imagine Jesus at a football game? Didn't He exhort his followers to "do unto others as you would have them do unto you"? Isn't the point of football to beat the other team by doing as much harm to the opposing players as possible?

Christianity has strayed about as far as it possibly can from its founder's ideas in many areas of life. Our Republican presidential candidate, George Bush Jr., who espouses Christian views and claims to be born again, is governor of the state with the highest rate of capital punishment in the country, a policy which most of the rest of the civilized world considers barbarian. This would receive Christ's blessing?

Imagine if Jesus returned to the world—as prophesized—and made a visit to New York City. Would he go around town in a stretch limousine or a bulletproof Popemobile visiting St. Patrick's Cathedral, the Fifth Ave. Presbyterian Church and the Cathedral of St. John the Divine—or would he take the subway to the nearest

AIDS hospice? I think the latter. "I came for the poor and the sick," He said.

I have heard people say it is impossible to lead a truly Christian life nowadays. On that point I must agree. But why, then, knowing this, do so many people nonetheless claim to be Christians —that is, followers of Christ? Can you imagine what a wonderful society this would be if all those who claimed to believe in God really did? If they really believed that He knew their every thought and was aware of their every action? The Postal Service would need extra trucks just to deliver the torrent of checks with donations for the churches.

Alas, as someone once said, the last true Christian died on the cross.

## Prayer at Football Games

The ongoing controversy over prayer at high school football games raises many questions in my mind. In the first place, does this God that everyone says they believe in really differentiate between the different forms of prayer? There are individual silent prayers, individual audible prayers, silent and audible group prayers and prayers led by a cleric of some sort. Does God pay more attention and respond to one kind more than others? Are prayers in church more pleasing to Him than others, for instance? As Jesus said, "Wheresoever two or three are gathered in my name, I am in the midst of them." According to this, any prayer at any time, in any place, is acceptable and legitimate.

What, then, is the purpose of prayer at football games? Is it just a group activity that appeals to believers? Who on Earth is fool enough to waste God's time by asking for victory in a football game? I can't actually imagine Jesus attending a football game—or even liking the sport at all. I suppose, then, that those who pray are asking that the players be protected from injury. Let's face it, though; football is a rough contact sport, and the aim, whether explicit or not, is partly to get the better opposing players off the field in any way possible, so there are no apologies if a few bloody noses or broken bones happen along the way. And honestly, if you don't want to get hurt, don't play football! A football player asking God for protection before a game makes no more sense than a skydiver asking Him for protection before engaging in that suicidal sport.

In an interesting twist, during a live TV broadcast of a professional game on December 13, 2010, a player, upon fumbling the ball and losing the game, was so humiliated he cried out in despair, "God did that to me!"

Update: The Times reported today (August 3, 2011) that a college player died as a result of head trauma received while playing football, and that 4 or 5 high school football players are killed each year from injuries sustained on the field.

Timothy Masters
Focus on The Family
Colorado Springs, CO 80995
September 20, 2003

Dear Mr. Masters:

We corresponded in the past once when I wrote to Rev. Dobson. I am a practicing psychiatrist and retired professor of psychiatry at Columbia Medical School in New York City. I know you are busy with many letters, but I am writing again in view of the fact that Dr. Dobson is now coming out against gay marriage and proposing legislation, perhaps even a constitutional amendment, to prohibit it.

I find this curious, since according to what I have read, some Catholic priests think that St. Paul was gay.

Meanwhile, I have been reading the Bible for my own edification. I have finished the New Testament and am halfway through the Old. What a collection of horror stories that is—with the Lord delivering whole cities to people like Joshua, who then proceeds to massacre everyone—men, women, and children! No wonder there is such mayhem in the Middle East—it has been going on for millennia!

Knowing that you people are interested in preserving the family, I wonder if you are aware that a major factor contributing to the demise of the family is the ease with which one can get a divorce nowadays. What about campaigning against divorce? In case you haven't read the Book of Matthew lately, Matthew 5:32 quotes Jesus as saying "But I say unto you, that whosoever shall put away his wife, saving for fornication, causeth her to commit *adultery* and whosoever shall marry her that is divorced committeth *adultery*" [my italics]. This is Jesus talking, Mr. Masters! And that's one of the Ten Commandments he's talking about! (Need I point out that there's no Commandment against homosexuality?)

What about supporting legislation or perhaps even a constitutional amendment prohibiting divorce? Let's face it, Mr. Masters, our country is a land of adulterers and adulteresses, isn't it? And as for fornication, that's going on all over, from teenagers to senior citizens in nursing homes. Why don't we hear you advocating legislation outlawing fornication?

As I have had occasion to point out to leaders of the Catholic Church, Jesus also had something to say about pedophilia. Matthew 18:6 reads "But whosoever shall offend one of these little ones who believeth in me, it were better for him that a millstone were hanged about his head and he be drowned in the depth of the sea." The very same bishops and priests who fail to take these words of Jesus seriously are now publicly refusing communion to politicians, such as Senator Kerry, who favor abortion rights for the rest of us! That's downright blackmail! And it's all the more galling because those men are in no position to judge anyone!

It is outrageous and hypocritical that religious leaders selectively quote scripture that appears to support their own particular moral leanings, while ignoring those rules that would be unpopular, to say the least, and would empty the pews in their churches and lose votes for the conservative politicians they support!

Timothy Masters
Focus on the Family
Colorado Springs, CO 80995
October 15, 2003

Dear Mr. Masters:

Thank you for your lengthy and interesting reply to my letter to Dr. Dobson. I realize you have lots of letters on your desk, and I appreciate your selecting mine to respond to.

In response to your points, let me assure you that I am quite familiar with Christianity, having been in my youth a devout Lutheran who planned to enter the clergy—that is, until I began thinking for myself and realized that Christian dogma completely ignored a great deal of the information and knowledge available to us in the twentieth century. For instance, I remember at my grandmother's funeral the pastor admonished our government for sending a man into space, on the grounds that "that was God's kingdom and we shouldn't invade it!" (Sputnik had just gone aloft.) He went on to explain to us that Grandma was at that moment up in heaven wearing white robes and that the book of her life was dripping with the blood of Jesus Christ. In spite of the occasion, I could hardly keep a straight face!

As for life after death, men of the church say "no Jesus, no heaven." Well, this is such nonsense. It seems quite clear to me that if there is any conscious existence at all after the death of the body everyone will participate equally. You Christians, meanwhile, would let only yourselves into Heaven, while telling everyone else to go to Hell—an awfully uncharitable attitude, I must say.

As for the Bible's teachings concerning homosexuality, everyone quotes the Book of Leviticus, where it is written that "mankind sleeping with mankind is an abomination." People don't often mention, however, that the text goes on to say that it's also an abomination to eat shrimp and other shellfish! Do you ever eat shrimp, Mr. Masters? Those rules were aimed at preventing disease, not moralizing.

It says in the Bible "Are not two sparrows sold for a farthing? Yet not one of them shall fall to the ground without your Father." Doesn't this mean that God is aware of the death of every living thing, no matter how small? If so, he must be aware of children dying of cancer, children having their arms and legs blown off in Iraq and all the rest of human misery. According to those two nuts Jimmy Falwell and Pat Robertson, that same God "let 9/11 happen" to punish America for its tolerance of abortion and homosexuality. Meanwhile, I recall that when abortions were illegal in this country, something like 15,000 women died each year from botched illegal abortions or self-administered abortions using a coat hanger. Do you advocate a return to those times?

Do Falwell and Robertson and their ilk really think that their God used Islamic terrorists to incinerate innocent people on 9/11? If so, they are plain crazy (In psychiatric terms one would say they are delusional with sadistic fantasies.) Franklin Graham agrees with them, by the way. Billy Graham, his father, had a plantation in the Carolinas that was guarded by Doberman pinschers and had a sign on the fence that said "Trespassers Will Be Eaten." Perhaps he had never heard of the Lord's Prayer. Are these men what you would call Christians, Mr. Masters?

And what about that verse that says "It is easier for a camel to go through the eye of a needle than for a rich man to enter the kingdom of Heaven"? I wonder how many clergymen mention this explicit biblical warning to their congregations—especially the ones in places like Park Avenue in New York City, for instance. Do you think that pious born-again Christian George W. Bush, our President, ever read that verse?

Jesus said, "Suffer the little children to come unto me, and forbid them not." If He "let 9/11 happen," does that mean that He also "let" his sexually infantilized priests abuse and destroy the lives of hundreds of children? And where was He while his bishops covered up those outrageous sins and crimes?

I hope I've given you something to ponder, although I suppose you've probably heard all of this before and your incredible powers of rationalization will protect you from doubts concerning your faith.

Thank you again for your letter.

## TO THE EDITOR OF THE NEW YORK TIMES:

## Miscarriages, God's Abortions

In "Roman Catholic War on Abortion" (May 9, 2009, p. A17) the subject of abortion is presented as the reason many Catholic clergy oppose the invitation extended to President Obama to speak at Notre Dame University. According to Roman Catholic beliefs, a fetus even at the earliest stage of development is a human life and is to be treated as such. Therefore, the argument goes, an abortion is equivalent to murder. Meanwhile, it is estimated that 15-20% of all pregnancies end in miscarriage, which is nothing more than a natural, spontaneous abortion. The Bible says, "Are not two sparrows sold for a farthing? Yet not one of them shall fall to the ground without your Father." From this we may assume that God is aware of the phenomenon of miscarriage and is, by His nature, a participant.

Furthermore, if all such fetuses are human beings, should they not be baptized and receive a Christian funeral and burial? I recall once as a medical student participating in a legal, medically indicated abortion in which the nurse in the operating room, inasmuch as the mother was Catholic, baptized the aborted specimen. This is of course not commonly done. Can Catholic theologians explain why miscarried and aborted fetuses are not routinely baptized if they are, in their view, full-fledged human beings?

# Jesus and Organized Religion

There has been great controversy recently over where houses of worship should and should not be built and it has revealed striking differences in the attitudes of various Christian denominations toward worship. In this connection there is an interesting passage in the New Testament suggesting that Jesus himself had definite views about organized religion. How else might one explain His admonition to worshippers in Matthew 6:5-13: "And when thou prayest, thou shalt not be as the hypocrites are: for they love to pray standing in the synagogues and in the corners of the streets, that they may be seen of men. Verily I say unto you, they have their reward. But thou, when thou prayest, enter into thy closet, and when thou hast shut the door, pray to thy Father which is in secret; and thy Father which seeth in secret shall reward thee openly. But when ye pray, use not vain repetitions, as the heathen do: for they think they shall be heard for their much speaking . . . After this manner, therefore pray ye: Our Father which art in heaven, Hallowed be thy name . . ." I wonder how many people have thought about the meaning of this passage?

It would really make a positive difference in the world if religious people would learn to tolerate those who don't share their particular beliefs or rituals. I think Jesus' own views on the matter are clear enough!

Then there's Mother Angelica, who with her group of young nuns say the rosary on TV for an hour or so each session. Do they really think that Mary wants to hear this prayer repeated perhaps thousands of times daily by people all over the world? I would think that with the thousands, if not millions, of individual personal prayers she has to listen to and deal with every day, all the Hail Marys must be a crashing bore and a real distraction.

Dr. James Dobson
Focus on the Family
Colorado Springs, CO
May 2007

Dear Dr. Dobson:

The other day you appeared on a TV news program commenting on the death of Rev. Jerry Falwell. You defended his anti-gay attitudes by stating that he was merely quoting scripture.

What about bigoted, angry evangelists who knowingly quote scripture in a highly selective manner to further their own power-hungry personal and political agendas? Now that's a real abomination—and a sad commentary on the present state of Christianity. Their views have no more to do with the teachings of Christ than do those of Franklin Graham, who, commenting on the perpetrator of the recent and tragic killings at Virginia Tech, voiced the opinion that the shooter was not mentally ill but rather "possessed by the devil." That places Graham right back in the 17th century at the Salem witch trials, I would say. Your inept quoting of Leviticus places you even further back in time—in the pre-Christian days of what are now called Kosher rules of hygiene. You guys really don't know what Christianity is all about, do you?

And have you heard the latest from that hostile, punishment-happy weirdo Pat Robertson, who claims that God told him that there would be a major terrorist attack in the United States this year involving thousands of victims? He's obviously either hallucinating or just making it up. Which do you think, Dr. Dobson? Do you think Rev. Robertson was actually spoken to by God—or is he just crazy?

## TO THE EDITOR OF THE NEW YORK TIMES:

## Some Embryonic Questions

In "Senate Chief Defies Bush On Stem Cells" (July 29, 2007, p. A1) it is reported that opponents of stem cell research, most of whom are conservative Christians, say that destroying human embryos is tantamount to murder. One is quoted as saying "An embryo is nascent human life."

I'd like to hear Christians who believe embryos are human beings answer the following questions:

Do embryos have souls?
Should all embryos be named and baptized?
Should attempts be made to keep laboratory-grown embryos alive,
    for instance by finding women willing to carry them to term?
When they die, should embryos be given Christian burials?
Do embryos go to heaven after they die?

Do these questions sound absurd? Well, so do the arguments made against stem cell research by conservative Christians and the politicians who pander to them.

## TO THE EDITOR OF THE NEW YORK TIMES:

## The Loaded 'God Question'

In his op-ed piece "The Religious Wars" Nicholas Kristof discusses two recent books on religion which, along with other recent books by Sam Harris, Richard Dawkins, and Christopher Hitchens, indicate an increasing interest in exploring the subject of religion and a new tendency among those who espouse the atheistic point of view to risk societal condemnation. Two traditional versions of the deity, the 'omniscient and omnipotent God' and the 'Grandpa in the sky,' along with other conventional beliefs, are questioned and attacked using a wide array of logical, psychological and scientific arguments. Dawkins accumulated enough contributions to his cause to pay for a sign on London busses that read "There probably is no God." In my opinion, it is time to replace the usual loaded question "Do you believe in God?" with "Do you believe there is a god?" The former contains the implicit assumption that there is in fact a deity known as God, and asks whether you believe in Him, while the latter asks the more basic question of whether you believe that such a thing as a god exists.

## TO THE EDITOR OF THE NEW YORK TIMES:

## Atheism is Not a Religion

In "And Now, Predictions We'll Back 100 Percent" (November 9, 2010, p. D8) one of the predictions is that "Atheism will not become a dominant world religion, despite the efforts of some scientists." What about the efforts of some disenchanted believers? In fact, there is just such a religion and it has been around for quite a while. It is called the Unitarian Universalist Association of Congregations (UUAC) and it is essentially a group made up mostly of formerly religious people of various faiths who welcome members of any religious group as well as humanists, pagans and atheists. (Atheists are actually mostly former believers who found that what they were told to believe was unbelievable. They disavow, for instance, the idea of the God the Father who had his son Jesus tortured to death in order to forgive all the sins that would be committed by people for the next few millennia.) The UUAC calls itself a 'non-deistic religion' and welcomes people with diverse beliefs about the possible presence of a higher power but doesn't require members to ascribe to any specific beliefs or dogma. Instead, members get together to share and discuss ideas about anything that might come under the general heading of the spiritual. It is at present the closest thing we have to an atheist religion. In my opinion, it would make an ideal world religion, and I hope someday that comes to pass.

## TO THE EDITOR OF THE NEW YORK TIMES:

### Reinhold Niebuhr, Where Are You Now?

When I saw the full page DefCon ad entitled "Meet America's Most Influential Stem Cell Scientists" (May 23, 2005, p. A1) I recalled a quote from Reinhold Niebuhr, the most famous theologian of the 20th century, who said that "Not much evil is done by evil men . . . Most of the evil is done by good people who do not know they are not good." I think this applies to all three of the angry religious leaders pictured in the article.

I then re-read Arthur Schlesinger's essay "Forgetting Reinhold Niebuhr" (Magazine Section, September 8, 2005), in which he asks, "Why, in an age of religiosity, has Niebuhr, the supreme American theologian of the 20th century, dropped out of 21st-century religious discourse? Maybe issues have taken more urgent forms since Niebuhr's death—terrorism, torture, abortion, same-sex marriage, Genesis versus Darwin, embryonic stem cell research. But maybe Niebuhr has fallen out of fashion because 9/11 has revived the myth of our national innocence. Lamentations about 'the end of innocence' became favorite clichés at the time." Schlesinger quotes a line by a character of Finley Peter Dunne to the effect that a fanatic "does what he thinks the Lord would do if He only knew the facts in the case" and goes on to paraphrase Niebuhr: "There is no greater human presumption than to read the mind of the Almighty, and no more dangerous individual than the one who has convinced himself that he is executing the Almighty's will. 'A democracy,' Niebuhr said, 'cannot of course engage in an explicit preventive war,' and he lamented the 'inability to comprehend the depth of evil to which individuals and communities may sink, particularly when they try to play the role of God to history.'"

Again quoting Niebuhr, he writes: "'Religion is so frequently a source of confusion in political life, and so frequently dangerous to democracy, precisely because it introduces absolutes into the realm of relative values.' Religion, he warned, could be a source of error as well as wisdom and light. Its role should be to inculcate, not a sense of infallibility, but a sense of humility. Indeed, 'the worst corruption is a corrupt religion.'"

"Like all God-fearing men, Americans are never safe 'against the temptation of claiming God too simply as the sanctifier of whatever we most fervently desire.'"

The article contains many other insights that are applicable to the present church vs. state debate and it would be very appropriate and worthwhile if the Times were to publish an editorial review of Schlesinger's essay.

## TO THE EDITOR OF THE NEW YORK TIMES:

## The Evolution of the God Gene

In "The Evolution of the God Gene" (November 15, 2009, p. 3) the author writes that atheists might be unwilling to accept the notion that religion is useful. To this I would reply that there doesn't have to be a God in order for religion to be useful, which of course it is! It provides opportunities for the expression of shared values and beliefs, social continuity and a certain degree of reassurance to help cope with the fear of death. At the same time, no one can deny the negatives associated with religious belief, chiefly the intolerance of other religions, up to and including the vilification and killing of 'infidels' and 'heretics' which has stoked countless religious wars over the ages.

The author goes on to say that those who believe in God may not welcome the idea that "the mind has been shaped to believe in gods" because then "the actual existence of the divine may then seem less likely." One way I've noticed that believers have of making sure such thoughts don't enter their minds is the phrasing of the basic question regarding religious belief: Do you believe in God? This question implicitly assumes God's existence as a fact and asks whether you believe in the God that is. A less manipulative way of putting the question would be: Do you believe there is a God?, since it allows for the possibility of there not being any God. Believers don't even want to contemplate such a possibility, so they naturally prefer the loaded version of the question. The doubts and fears that the religiously faithful cover up by means of this linguistic dodge are the reason they have such strong negative feelings toward atheists. This also explains why it is unthinkable that an atheist could ever be elected President of the United States: it would raise the question of whether God exists at all too uncomfortably for too many people.

## TO THE EDITOR OF THE NEW YORK TIMES:

### Atheism and Christianity

Public discussions on the subject of religion have become ubiquitous in our society, especially in politics, education and the media. This has been accompanied in particular by authors taking increasing notice of atheism, for example in such books as Harold Dawkins's *The God Delusion* and Sam Harris's *The End of Faith* and *Letter to a Christian Nation*. A propos of atheism, interest in its influence is growing and there are even atheist groups and societies. I would like to contend that there isn't much difference between Christians and atheists, with the main difference being that Christians either don't realize how little they really believe of what they say they believe, or are afraid to admit it.

Atheists are viewed in our society with disapproval, suspicion and contempt. They are considered less moral and trustworthy than the religious. They are seen as having abandoned their faith and therefore as anti-Christian, despite the fact that atheists rarely try to convert anyone to atheism. Still, no atheist could ever be elected President of the United States, so the candidates for that office dutifully announce what they call their respective 'faiths,' while carefully avoiding any discussion of specifics.

As a youngster in Sunday school at a very conservative Protestant church, I was taught that there is a being called God who is omniscient, omnipotent and omnipresent—which I take it is the belief held by most Christian denominations. If we assume that God is omniscient and silent prayers are received by the Deity, it follows that our brains are being monitored 24 hours a day from cradle to grave and all our thoughts, feelings, and behavior are being stored in some sort of heavenly computer until we die, at which time the information will be used to determine our fate for eternity.

Certainly American society is not a good example of adherence to Christian morality. Jimmy Carter apparently once said that "If you lust in your heart for someone, you are committing adultery." Meanwhile, a study was done some years ago in which it was shown that college men had a sexual thought every 20 seconds. From this it would follow that most men are committing adultery most of the time. Adultery, of course, is the subject of one of the Ten Commandments. Jesus himself says in three places in the Bible that anyone who marries a divorced person is committing adultery. Well, that takes care of half the population right there. (Paradoxically, the divorce rate is higher in the so-called Bible Belt.) The other half, those who have had any kind of sexual relations outside of marriage of any kind, are fornicators, something which is also strictly forbidden by the Bible, notably by St. Paul.

Or take the matter of tithing. According to the Bible, the faithful are supposed to donate ten percent of their income to the church. I doubt most churchgoers hold to this rule. If they did really believe (if they *knew*) that God was aware of their donations, they would all tithe religiously, so to speak, and churches wouldn't need to organize any more suppers to raise money for building repairs. Plenty of people would donate far more than ten percent in order to appear especially charitable to their God. As the Bible makes clear, of all the virtues the most important is charity.

In sum, if Christians really believed what they claim to believe, churches would be rich, popular and crowded and the clergy would be in demand everywhere as guests and counselors and would be indispensable allies for politicians. People would really try their best to be models of good behavior, charitable, benevolent, forgiving and helpful. There would be no cheating in business or in play, no domestic violence; and charity, sacrifice and devotion to the general welfare would be the rule rather than the exception.

One could object that this would be expecting too much of human nature, given what we know it to be, with its frailties and darker sides. But if religious beliefs were not just possibilities, but absolute truths—if people really believed and *knew* them to be true—these ideals would be the universal order of the day and everyone would practice them without thinking twice. But the fact that no one can actually *know* whether God, heaven, the afterlife, etc. are true, only the very few are willing to live *as if they were*. There is too much doubt inherent in any belief system to expect it to be accepted and lived by large numbers of people as absolute truth.

For me, the real question is, why does God remain hidden and silent? Why does He not reveal Himself so that people would have no reason to doubt or hesitate about doing what was morally right and good? In the Old Testament we read of actual conversations He had with His followers. Then, in the New Testament, this all stopped. Even Mother Theresa towards the end of her life admitted that she had at times questioned her faith. Atheists are merely saying that they cannot believe in religious dogma when so few facts of life support it.

## Believers vs. Unbelievers

Christians who believe that there is a God the Father and God the Son in Heaven up in the sky somewhere find it difficult to accept the fact that there are people who do not share these beliefs and that these people might be right. Inasmuch as there is no tangible evidence to prove the existence of a God, varying degrees of doubt pervade religious communities, and the mere existence of unbelievers is a constant threat to their convictions. In earlier times, Christians didn't think twice about torturing unbelievers and heretics and calmly burned them the stake. Religious persecution has been around as long as religion, and it continues in full force all over the world. In my view, most of the world's troubles today are the result of religious intolerance. Christians want to convert everyone to their way of thinking and beliefs, and Muslims want to kill the 'infidels' and make the world into an Islamic theocracy.

Islamic extremists are killing as many innocent non-Muslims as they can right now, and believe it is their God's will. Although Christians are not at present systematically torturing and killing non-Christians, they still engage in a sort of persecution of atheists, whom they condemn, socially ostracize and hold in contempt for being amoral or even evil. The idea of tolerating a group of intelligent, moral and humanistic people who do not share their religious beliefs is beyond their ken. Not only that, but Christian belief, which is held by only about a third of the world's population, condemns the rest of humanity to eternal damnation and fiery torture in what Christians call Hell. Religious extremists of whatever stripe are dangerous people because, as Reinhold Niebuhr noted, "religious fanaticism is rooted in doubt."

Fundamentalist Christians in this country are gaining in political power and are attempting to make Christianity the national religion by requiring that Christian ideas and prayer be taught in schools and other tokens of Christian beliefs be part of our public lives. The idea that there are people who do not want their children to be taught that Christianity is absolute truth is anathema to Christians. They will never be able to accept the possibility that others have a right to their own beliefs or to deny the existence of God—it is too much of a threat to their own shaky belief system.

## TO THE EDITOR OF THE NEW YORK TIMES:

## The New Shrine to Our Lady of Good Help

In "Wisconsin Is Put on the Map to Pray With the Virgin Mary" (December 24, 2010, p. A1) we read a description of a new Catholic shrine to Our Lady of Good Help, where apparitions of the Virgin Mary have been officially validated by the Roman Catholic Church. The decision was based on a statement by a local parishioner, a certain Adele Brice, who reported in 1858 that she had had been visited three times by Mary "who hovered between two trees in a bright light, clothed in dazzling white with a yellow sash around her waist and a crown of stars above her flowing blond locks." Wow! Who could ever doubt the authenticity of such a sighting?

After two years of investigations, the local bishop "stated with moral certainty" that Miss Brice had indeed had encounters of a "supernatural character" that were "worthy of belief." One Bishop later opined, "It would be devious to say that this was somehow pulled out of the attic to exorcise the problems of the church today." Who would ever say such a thing? After all, why couldn't the Virgin Mary have visited Champion, Wisconsin? (And the Catholic Church is wondering why it is losing followers and having to close churches because of low attendance!)

Bill O'Reilly
Fox News
December 2009

Dear Bill,

On your show last night you commented on the American Humanist Association's recent sponsorship of bus advertisements featuring statements such as 'There probably is No God,' saying they were jealous because they didn't have a baby to celebrate on Christmas. Well, allow me to point out that atheists have come to the conclusion that no one, not even the Pope, knows any more about whether there is a God or an afterlife than a newborn baby does. Given the impossibility of knowing, the probability of there being a God is 50-50, that is, there either is or isn't one. The common question Do you believe in God? is a loaded question because what it is really means is: There is a God; do you believe in Him?

In my opinion, Christians have such strong negative feelings toward atheists because the mere existence of skeptical people plants a seed of doubt in their minds about religious belief generally. As Reinhold Niebuhr, the famous theologian, said: "Religious fanaticism is rooted in doubt." Christians act like they have a monopoly on goodness, morality and the human virtues. In fact, vast numbers of Christians, like people of other religions throughout history, have been guilty of gross intolerance and hatred and of committing violence and waging wars to eliminate heretics and nonbelievers—all in an attempt to maintain their own beliefs free from doubt. It is deeply ironic that in their desperation to do so they resort to morally repugnant actions. In the recent past, Catholics and Protestants in Northern Ireland were killing each other's children in the name of religion.

Atheists have no need to go to such lengths to defend their views. The atheist position simply amounts to saying something like the following: I don't think that there is a god—certainly not the loving God the Father in heaven that believers talk about—since I see no concrete evidence that such a being exists. Indeed, most of what goes on in this world suggests that there is no benevolent God, or else there wouldn't be wars, massacres, genocides, diseases, cancer, horrendous birth defects and all the other evils and suffering to which humans are prone. Therefore, either your God doesn't care about the human condition and won't do anything about it, or he can't do anything about it, or there is no God.

As Jackie Kennedy Onassis said shortly before her death, "If there is a God, he's cruel." She should know!

# TO THE EDITOR OF THE NEW YORK TIMES:

## End-of-World Predictions

In "Pastor Stirs Wrath with His Views on Old Questions" (March 5, 2011, p. A12) a leading evangelical pastor questions the fundamentalist belief that following the destruction and end of the world only faithful Christians will be taken into eternal life in Heaven and the rest of the world will end up in eternal damnation in Hell. (Harold Camping of Open Forum says it's going to happen on April 21, 2011) Well, I'd like to point out that this God they talk about already did this once before, and you can read about it in the Old Testament story in which the whole world was destroyed by flood except for the lucky ones on Noah's Ark. This God must really hate the world if he plans to do the same thing again, condemning the vast majority of its population to eternal fire in Hell! In another article in today's Times, "New Cases Loom in Priest Scandal," (p. A1) we read of the continuing scandal in the Roman Catholic Church involving the alleged cover-up by bishops of the circumstances surrounding 37 priests accused of sexually abusing minors—this in spite of all the publicity and discussion of this evil that has scandalized the world for years now. Why, might I ask, does their God let this happen? Is it not curious, not to say outrageous, that the God worshipped by Christians allows his representatives on Earth to continue this destructive, criminal behavior and hates the rest of us so much that he plans to destroy us all for a second time?

Harold Camping's new date for the end of the world is October 21, 2011.

## TO THE EDITOR OF THE NEW YORK TIMES:

### The Cross at Ground Zero

In "Atheists Sue to Block Display of Cross-Shaped Trade Center Beam in 9/11 Museum" (July 29, 2001, page A20) we read about the controversy over a cross-shaped beam discovered in the debris at the World Trade Center. A Catholic priest was shown on TV news splashing holy water on the object and the plan is to install it in the museum as a part of the memorial. People have already raised objections based on the principle of separation of church and state. I would like to note that, from a secular perspective, the cross was an instrument of torture and execution in the first century. In our culture it symbolizes the sacrifice of Jesus Christ, required of him by his Father in heaven, so that the sins of those who believed in him would be forgiven. If Christ had lived in the 20th century and had been executed by a present-day method such as the electric chair, would that mean that models of an electric chair would be displayed on church steeples and altars and his followers would hang miniature gold electric chairs around their necks? Would congregations sing a hymn called "The Old Rugged Chair, the Dearest and Best"? If he had been hung instead, would churches display hangman's nooses and sing "The Old Rugged Noose"?

## TO THE EDITOR OF THE NEW YORK TIMES:

### Selective Christian (Im)morality

In "Rights Collide as Town Clerk Sidesteps Role in Gay Marriages" (September 28, 2011, front page) it is reported that Rose Marie Belforti, the elected town clerk of Ledyard, N.Y., refuses to sign marriage certificates for same-sex couples on the grounds that

God considers homosexuality a sin. She cites a passage in Romans, in which, she says, homosexuality is condemned. Perhaps Ms. Belforti has never read the Matthew 5:32, in which Jesus himself says "Whosoever shall put away his wife, saving for the cause of fornication, causeth her to commit adultery: and whosoever shall marry her that is divorced committeth adultery." In Mark 10:11 he says again "Whosoever shall put away his wife and marry another, committeth adultery against her." Now as I recall, among the first things we learned in Sunday School were the Ten Commandments, one of which is "Thou shall not commit adultery." I wonder whether Ms. Belforti has been willing to sign marriage certificates for divorced people who remarry? To my knowledge, Jesus never said anything about homosexuality.

## TO THE EDITOR OF THE NEW YORK TIMES:

## Religion and Politics at Their Worst

In "Prominent Pastor Calls Romney's Church a Cult" (October 8, 2011, p. A10) it is reported that the Texas evangelist Pastor Robert Jeffress referred to the Mormon religion as a "cult" and asserted that it was not really Christian. He claims that "this has been the historical position of Christianity for a long time . . . Most people—even evangelical Christians—don't want to admit that they have a problem with Mormonism. They think it is bigoted to say so." I have news for you, Mr. Jeffress. The reason that they, along with everyone else, think it is bigoted is because *it is*!

Evangelical Christians seem to be intolerant of everyone who doesn't agree with them. Of course, as far as they are concerned, everyone else is going to Hell anyway. This, to my mind, is not very Christian. Historians have described Jesus himself as a "cult hero." I wonder what Jeffress thinks of Martin Luther and the Lutheran Church?

# Chapter 5

## CATHOLIC BISHOPS
## AND PRIESTS

T HE TOPIC OF THIS CHAPTER is the scandal in the Catholic Church surrounding the many cases which have recently come to light involving sexual abuse of children committed by Catholic bishops and priests dating back to the 1960s and 1970s. These incidents have surfaced and attracted widespread attention only in the last couple of years and have already resulted in a barrage of legal cases, convictions and large monetary awards. The media has been full of stories from all over the world in which victims who were molested by clergymen as children have won substantial awards in cases where guilt has been determined. Sympathy and support groups have formed for abuse victims as they come forward to accuse specific clergymen and fight for justice not only in the offices of the Church, but also in the courts. Bishops who mishandled case after case by transferring errant clergy to other parishes have offered apologies. Only recently, however, have Church authorities admitted that they have been handling the problem of pedophilia as a sin rather than as a heinous crime rooted in deep psychopathology. The following are responses to some of the more informative and often shocking articles that have appeared in the press. Also included are letters addressed to prominent Roman Catholic leaders.

*　　*　　*

# TO THE EDITOR OF THE NEW YORK TIMES:

## Even the Pope Doesn't Get It

The Pope was quoted in the New York Times as saying that the Catholic Church must "address the sin of abuse within the wider context of sexual mores." What the Pope doesn't get is that while the sexual abuse of children is viewed by him and the Church in terms of sin, the rest of society condemns this evil least of all for its sinfulness. In the United States, sexual abuse of children is a felony crime punishable by imprisonment. It is devastating for the child victims, often causing lifelong psychological damage. By referring to it as 'the sin of abuse' and thereby reducing it to a religious infraction, the Pope reveals his own ignorance of human psychosexual development and blindness to the psychological trauma inflicted upon thousands of children by pedophile priests. Even the use of the word 'scandal' is another way in which the church is attempting to minimize the disastrous effects of the problem. As Jesus said, "Anyone who would harm one of these little ones, who believeth in me, it would better a millstone be tied around his neck and he be cast into the depths of the sea." In other words, by using these and other euphemisms, the Catholic Church comes dangerously close to condoning criminal behavior.

Cardinal John O'Connor
St Patrick's Cathedral
New York, N.Y.
June 3, 1998

Dear Cardinal O'Connor:

No doubt you have seen the article in today's New York Times reporting the resignation of Bishop Symons following his admission that he was a pedophile and had molested several young boys in his parish years ago. His statements struck me as yet another indication that Roman Catholic clergy in general and the leadership of the Church in particular are abysmally ignorant when it comes to human psychological development and specifically human sexual development.

Bishop Symons's successor, Bishop Lynch, is quoted in the article as follows: "Pedophilia wasn't even in the psychological manuals when this abuse happened. The old theory was, 'Make a good confession and sin no more.' We never realized it was a disease. It wasn't in our manuals." Are we to understand from this that it didn't occur to anyone in the Church that this was child molestation and that no one stopped to consider what it did to the young victims? These appalling comments deserve your thoughtful attention, Cardinal O'Connor.

Are we honestly to believe that only 25 years ago Catholic clergy were literally unaware that pedophilia was an abnormal condition and the sexual abuse of children a crime? If so, are we to infer from this that it was considered normal? Were your "psychological manuals" so outdated, so prehistoric, that they made no mention of this highly pathological and severely damaging behavior? Are we to understand that the Church regarded this behavior as no more than a minor sin, punishable by a slap on the wrist, then to be absolved and hidden by simply transferring the offending priest to a distant parish and other unsuspecting parents and children? Were your clergy not aware of the likelihood that this behavior would inflict permanent psychological damage on the child victims?

If your answer is yes to any of these questions, then the Catholic Church is guilty of gross negligence and appalling ignorance and naïveté when it comes to human psychology. The fact that the Church may choose to view child molestation as a minor infraction of its rules in no way exonerates your clergy for their unpardonable behavior. (Parishioners are routinely excommunicated from the church for far less serious offenses.)

Medical doctors who are discovered to have sexually abused their patients are not only stripped of their licenses, but may be criminally prosecuted and, if found guilty, jailed. If a member of the Catholic clergy raped an adult woman, would the Church recognize that as a criminal offense, or would it view that, too, merely as a sin requiring nothing more than confession and penance to absolve the perpetrator's guilt? Are you and your Church not aware that the sexual abuse of children is far more damaging and therefore reprehensible than even the rape of an adult?

One could go a step further and hypothesize that the global denial by the Church of the implications of pedophilic predation among its clergy may be the result of two mutually reinforcing factors. First, it may be that pedophilia is, in fact, so prevalent among the clergy that perpetrators are protected because there are many other clergy who feel it is acceptable. Second, it may be that the church, concerned over declining numbers of priests generally, is not interested in reducing the numbers further by weeding out pedophiles. As a result, pedophilia has become an institutionally tolerated condition, an object of denial which is reflexively downplayed and hushed up.

You moralize about other people's behavior—divorce, extramarital sexuality and homosexuality—but you had better look to your own house. From a moral standpoint, these are minor matters compared with the evil perpetrated over the years against children by Catholic clergy.

If the Church doesn't start learning about human psychology and psychosexual development and bring itself at least into the twentieth century (even though the rest of the world is now entering the twenty-first), it will just fall more and more hopelessly behind the times.

I had planned to write about this in a letter to the editor of the New York Times, but I decided it would not have much effect apart from prompting an attack on me for criticizing the Catholic Church. This is the usual way the Church defends itself against criticism. You take the attitude that the Church can do no wrong and only it can judge itself. Well, hear it from me: in this case the Catholic Church is guilty of inexcusable attitudes and unpardonable crimes.

I am a practicing psychiatrist here in New York City and an interested observer of what goes on in the city. I am well aware of your opinions and attitudes towards groups which you assail for behavior you consider sinful. As your Savior said on one of the very few occasions when he spoke about people who would *judge the sexual behavior of others*, "Let he who is without sin cast the first stone." De te fabula narratur!

Unless I am mistaken, Jesus never said a word about homosexuality or any kind of sexuality, for that matter. Those who condemn homosexuality cite passages from the book of Leviticus where it is called an abomination. Well, according to the same passage in Leviticus it's also an abomination to eat shrimp! Do you eat shrimp, Cardinal O'Connor?

[Cardinal John O'Connor was Archbishop of New York from 1990 until his death at the age of 80 in 2000. He was a well known and highly regarded Catholic leader and spokesperson.]

Bishop Thomas Tobin
Archdiocese of Providence
One Cathedral Square
Providence, R.I. 02903
December 2, 2009

Dear Bishop Tobin:

Having just listened to your conversation with Bill O'Reilly on Fox News this evening, I couldn't resist writing to you and sharing some thoughts on the subjects you discussed. As to abortion, I am an M.D. whose training and early years of practice came before Roe v. Wade. At that time, approximately 15,000 women died each year in the United States from botched illegal or self-induced (coat hanger) abortions. This means that in the 35 years since Roe v. Wade over 500,000 women's lives have been saved. This statistic is conspicuous by its absence in the debate over abortion. Is it the Roman Catholic Church's position that saving the lives of all unborn fetuses is more important than saving the lives of adult women?

If fetuses are living beings, why doesn't the Church take the position that each one must be baptized and given a Christian burial? When I was doing my residency, I recall once in a hospital seeing a nurse baptize the fetus after a life-saving abortion in the operating room. Was she correct or not?

What about unused living embryos, which are usually thrown in a medical waste receptacle. Human beings, you say?

Bill O'Reilly asked you at one point whether you would deny Communion to those who engage in what you consider immoral sexual practices. You avoided answering that question. According to scripture, Jesus himself stated in three places that anyone who marries a divorced person is committing adultery, thereby violating one of the Ten Commandments. Would you also deny these people Communion or require that they remain unmarried and desist from all sexual activity?

Like the Roman Catholic Church, most other Christian churches (except for the Episcopal Church) consider homosexual relationships immoral and sinful. Homosexuals are condemned for their behavior, and yet people who divorce and remarry are not, even though the Bible condemns their sexual behavior as adulterous. How do you justify such a selective approach to sin? My impression is that if churches did forbid the remarried divorced from being sexually active, or came out and clearly said they were living in sin, congregations would shrink dramatically. In any case, no one here in the U.S. would pay any attention to what any church had to say on the subject, just as in Europe, they don't.

My question really boils down to this. Senator Kennedy supports legislation which, the Catholic Church's opposition notwithstanding, is in the interests of his entire constituency, many of whom feel that it should be a woman's right to choose to have an abortion. How can the Church condemn him for this, when it itself is so inconsistent in its view of what is and is not sin? Your position that an abortion should not be performed even in cases of rape or incest—and, apparently, even to save the life of the woman—is cruel to the point of being inhumane. I doubt Jesus would agree with you.

But then again, as Jackie Onassis Kennedy said shortly before her death, "If there is a God, he's cruel." She would know! Apparently some of the Kennedys are not so sympathetic to your Church.

Sincerely Yours,

## TO THE EDITOR OF THE NEW YORK TIMES:

### They Still Don't Get It,
### But Keating Does and They Don't Like It

In "Head of Priest Abuse Panel Draws Ire With Comments" (June 14, 2003, p. A10) we read that former Oklahoma Governor Frank Keating's remark that "some unnamed members of the Church's hierarchy were acting like La Cosa Nostra" elicited this response from Tom Tamberg, spokesman for the local archdiocese: "Comparing the Church to an organization that kills and deals drugs—that is just way out of line." Apparently Tom Tamberg thinks that murder and drug dealing are worse crimes than sexually molesting and raping children. Coincidentally, there was another article that day in the paper (p. B6) from which we may conclude that Judge Alan H. Nevas in Bridgeport, Connecticut, would disagree with Tamberg. In sentencing the three-term mayor of Waterbury, CT, and United States Senate candidate to 37 years in prison for having sexually abused young girls while in office, Judge Nevas remarked that in his 18 years on the federal bench trying murderers and drug dealers, "this case was the worst I've ever seen." So for one federal judge at least, the comparison is not out of line at all. Let's face it: Keating is right.

## TO THE EDITOR OF THE RECORD:

### Governor McGreevey and the Bishops

In "McGreevey Won't Take Communion in Public" (November 19, 2010) it is reported that Catholic bishops are denying Communion to the Governor for his stand in support of abortion rights in New Jersey.

Congratulations to the Governor for resisting blackmail by bishops who are trying to impose their religious dogma on the rest of us. They like to focus on protecting the unborn, but where were they when already born children needed them? Whatever sins the Governor may have committed, they will undoubtedly be forgiven by whatever God there is, who recalls, as I do, the days when abortion was illegal in America and thousands of pregnant women died from botched, illegal and even self-inflicted coat hanger abortions. McGreevey will be rewarded for his courageous and selfless stand and one hopes that his example will be followed by other Catholic elected officials. By the way, the former Governor is now working towards being an Episcopal priest.

## TO THE EDITOR OF THE NEW YORK TIMES: JUNE 16, 2002

### Pedophilic Behavior and Its Problems

There are several articles in today's Times that raise the question of how the Catholic Church should deal with pedophilic behavior (sexual assault on children) by priests. The answer is easy and obvious. The Church should deal with it in the same way it would deal with the rape of an adult woman by a priest, because both crimes are of the same order. They both involve knowingly inflicting severe psychological damage on innocent victims and should be treated with zero tolerance anywhere—in or out of the Church. I actually doubt that active rapists of adults would have been transferred to other parishes, as child molesters have been in the past. The Church denied the seriousness of sexual assault of children in an effort to protect and retain pedophile priests in their midst and to avoid the sort of scandal in which they are now embroiled. The Catholic Church needs to start treating these crimes the way the rest of society does, period.

## TO THE EDITOR OF THE NEW YORK TIMES:

Catholic bishops continue to debate how best to eliminate active pedophiles from the clergy, but the bishops are in denial concerning the root of the problem, namely the presence among the clergy of significant numbers of priests with a pedophilic sexual orientation, which in psychiatric terms is a diagnosable condition that comes under the heading of paraphilia—the need for unusual sexual stimulation. Whether a given priest has acted out impulses of this kind by sexually molesting a child many times, once or never is actually irrelevant. Anyone with this orientation is at high risk for eventually engaging in active pedophilic behavior. One incidence of sexual molestation is enough to make the diagnosis of this condition. This is because mature, sexually well-adjusted adults just don't molest children—they find it abhorrent. Priests with this condition should be identified before they commit an offense. Instead, the Church waits until these horrors occur and then debates whether there is sufficient evidence to take action.

## TO THE EDITOR OF THE NEW YORK TIMES:

Today's article "Vatican to Hold Secret Trials of Priests in Pedophilia Cases" is yet one more example proving that, in the words of one American church official, "They just don't get it." The Pope has characterized pedophilia as one of the graver offenses against Church law, but this, too, misses the point entirely. Sexual abuse of children is a crime. It is just as traumatic and devastating to the child victim as rape is to the adult victim, if not more so, and should be treated as a crime of the same seriousness. This is what they "don't get": the Catholic Church sees pedophilia as a sin, whereas in fact it is a crime.

# TO THE EDITOR OF THE NEW YORK TIMES: MARCH 2002

## Sins—Or Sex Crimes Against Children?

The recent articles and discussions about the so-called scandal in the Catholic Church emphasize the pedophilic behavior of individual priests and the repeated cover-ups of this activity by bishops, both of which have been disastrous for the Church and for the innocent child victims. However, the real scandal in my opinion is priests' ignorance of and refusal to acknowledge what the rest of society has learned about human psychosexual development, sexual psychopathology and the effects of sexual molestation and assault on victims. This all the more disturbing, since priests play their role in locus parentis, which only adds to the already severe psychological trauma experienced by their victims.

The Catholic Church has never welcomed the insights of Freudian psychoanalysis or other psychological theories, fearing that they would undermine the teachings of the Church. The Church, for its part, does not see pedophilia as either pathological or criminal; if it did, we would see the Church handle it differently. For the Church, pedophilia is merely immoral, similar to but not as reprehensible as other forms of extramarital sexual conduct. For instance, Catholics who divorce and then remarry are treated as having committed a much more serious infraction against the Church's rules and are often excommunicated. Child molesting priests, on the other hand, need not fear this punishment—they are merely counseled to control their urges and "sin no more."

Just last week, in connection with the molestation of children by clergy, Bishop Thomas V. Daily of Brooklyn was quoted as saying, in effect, "We didn't ask enough questions or get more details—we just didn't do that in those days." The Times has also reported (March 11, 2002, p. B7) that Archbishop Daniel A. Cronin of Hartford, in response to misconduct by priests under his jurisdiction, said that "immoral activity of this nature is reprehensible and in no way tolerated or condoned." Bishop Law of Boston recently "apologized" for his handling of Father John Geoghan, a priest whose extensive sexual abuse of children became known to Law and whom the bishop merely reassigned to other parishes. Geoghan allegedly victimized over 100 children before he was finally convicted and put in prison—where he was eventually murdered.

In none of these cases do we see any evidence that Church leaders are aware that what they call "immoral activity" is really sexual assault—in many cases rape—and that, in addition to being devastating to the child victims and clearly indicative of psychopathology in the perpetrators, it is a felony crime. To these bishops, the crimes committed by the priests under their supervision were merely "immoral," and it is enough now to "apologize" for failing to take their crimes seriously, repeatedly covering them up and transferring the known offenders to other parishes—and other innocent victims.

## A Possible Clue to the Presence of Pedophilia in the Catholic Clergy

Bishop Fulton Sheen was a very popular and telegenic Catholic clergyman who lectured and preached to large TV audiences from 1952 to 1957. He was particularly outspoken in his criticism of Freud and those who shared his psychoanalytic theories about infantile sexuality. He stated that the only psychiatrist whose views he agreed with was a certain Roman Catholic psychiatrist on the staff of St. Luke's Hospital in New York City. He completely derided and rejected the idea that sexuality began early in life and such concepts as the Oedipus complex, etc. This, we now see clearly, had the effect of giving clergy a green light to engage in sexual behavior with children, for if children could not possibly experience sexual arousal, how could it be harmful? Thus Cardinal Law of Boston would make the following entry in the personnel file of one of his priests: "*He fools around with children*"—as if it were totally harmless, almost cute.

By all appearances, Bishop Sheen's views have had quite an influence over the years on the psychological training of Catholic clergy, which has ignored developments in our knowledge and awareness that children are in fact sexual beings and can be seriously and irrevocably traumatized by inappropriate sexual contact.

## TO THE EDITOR OF THE NEW YORK TIMES:

## The Other Side of Sexual Abuse in the Catholic Church

Much has been written about sexual abuse of children by Catholic priests, but little has been written about the abuse of seminarians by the Catholic Church. The reproductive impulse is perhaps the strongest of human drives, and the systematic attempts to suppress it in seminary students is tantamount to psychological castration and no doubt interferes with their overall emotional development. It would be like forbidding hunger and insisting that young men be satisfied with a lifelong diet of bread and water and that they profess to like it. It is like saying, in effect, "You must not have an adult male sex drive, you must repress the urge to reproduce and you must have no sex life at all—or you have sinned." The result, as we see, is a total stunting of psychosexual development that leaves young men at the developmental level of children. In fact, the Catholic Church wants these men to be and to identify themselves in large part as children. Pedophilia among priests is only the symptom, not the problem. A person's sexual drive cannot be eliminated without major consequences—pedophilia or other psychological disorders or rebellion against rules (the last being the healthiest.) The Catholic Church's dogma, rules and administrative policies are the problem and the priests are the first victims.

## TO THE EDITOR OF THE NEW YORK TIMES:

## The Vatican and Pedophilia—They Still Don't Get It

In "Vatican Revises Sexual Abuse Process but Causes Stir" (July 17, 2010) we read that in the Catholic Church the ordination of women appears on a list of "delicts, or offenses" together with pedophilia, heresy, apostasy and schism. A Vatican Monsignor goes on record with the pronouncement that "sexual abuse and pornography are more grave delicts—they are egregious violation of moral law." To my mind, declaring that the sexual abuse of children is a violation of moral law and sinful doesn't come close to capturing why it is evil. It is because the men of the Church have no clue and don't care that one rarely hears them mention the severe psychological damage these crimes cause in victims or the severe psychopathology of the priests involved. The reason is simple: throughout the past, pedophilia was viewed by the Church as neither pathological nor criminal. And even today the subject is discussed only in terms of morality and sin because that is all that interests the Catholic Church. To learn Jesus' thoughts on the subject, we need only consult Mark 18:6, where we read "Whoso shall offend one of these little ones which believe in me, it were better for him that a millstone were hanged about his neck and that he were drowned in the depth of the sea." Was he referring to pedophilia?

## TO THE EDITOR OF THE NEW YORK TIMES:

## The Vatican on Aggressive Atheism

In "The Vatican: Cardinal Cancels Trip" it is reported that Cardinal Walter Kasper cancelled his plan to accompany Pope

Benedict XVI on a trip to England, citing that country's "aggressive atheism." What about the Vatican's and the Pope's aggressive Christianity? The Pope regularly criticizes European countries for their secularism, admonishing them to return to Christianity. For the Catholic Church atheism is a derogatory term that refers to something sinful and evil, and atheists in its view are damned to go to Hell. Atheists themselves, on the other hand, consider themselves to be neither sinful, nor evil or even immoral, but rather realistic, informed and liberated from belief in religious dogma. Neither do they try to change the minds of believers, Christian or otherwise. The fact is, the Pope doesn't know any more about the existence of a god or what happens after death than does a newborn baby. The probability of there being a God as He is imagined in the Christian belief system is 50/50—either there is a God or there isn't.

## TO THE EDITOR OF THE NEW YORK TIMES:

## The Question of Married Priests and Bishops

In "Catholic Bishops Again Reject Married Priests" (October 19, 2002) it is reported that the question of whether to allow clergy to marry was once again discussed in the Catholic Church and once again rejected. One of the bishops refers to celibacy as "the crown jewel of Catholicism." Meanwhile, articles in the past have reported dissenting opinions, including at least one Catholic clergyman who believes celibacy has no theological foundation whatsoever. The Bible, meanwhile, is quite clear on the matter. In 1st Timothy 3:1 Paul says "This is a true saying, If a man desire the office of a bishop, he desireth a good work. A bishop then must be blameless, the husband of one wife, vigilant, sober, of good behavior, given to hospitality, apt to teach; . . . One that ruleth well his own house, having his children in subjection with all gravity; (For if a man know not how to rule his own house, how shall he take care of the church of God?)" He then goes on to suggest the same qualifications for deacons. I wonder why these passages are never quoted? The celibacy requirement for priests and bishops is obviously not based on the Bible.

## TO THE EDITOR OF THE NEW YORK TIMES:

### Female and Married Male Priests; Or, the Vatican's Fatal Mistake

In an article under the headline "In 3 Countries, Challenging the Vatican on Female Priests" (July 23, 2011, front page) it is reported that there is a growing movement in the Catholic Church to allow the ordination of women and married men. The Vatican's response to the ordination of women until now has been automatic excommunication, a position which it justifies by citing the fact that the apostles of Jesus Christ were all men. Meanwhile, it must be obvious to everyone, including even the Vatican, that had the Catholic Church reversed its stubborn refusal to ordinate women and married men, it in all probability would have spared itself the ruinous and self-destructive scandal of the past several years and, more importantly, would have spared thousand of children the psychological damage inflicted on them by its celibate clergy. I can't imagine that the God Catholics worship would support the Vatican's position.

## TO THE EDITOR OF THE NEW YORK TIMES:

### Who Killed John Geoghan?

As reported in the Times, former Catholic priest John Geoghan was murdered by a fellow inmate of the prison where he was serving a 9-10 year sentence for child molestation. In my view, the real killers of this wretched man were the Catholic bishops who enabled him to continue his lengthy spree of felony sex crimes unhindered. The Catholic Church has long refused to give any credence to modern psychological insights, in particular those of Sigmund Freud and his theories of infantile sexuality. It is these Catholic bishops' abysmal ignorance of human psychology—and of human sexuality, its perversions and the psychological devastation that pedophiles can inflict on their victims—that allowed Geoghan to continue on a path of self-destruction while inflicting various degrees of emotional trauma on well over a hundred children.

## TO THE EDITOR OF THE NEW YORK TIMES:

## On the Zero-Tolerance Rule

Today's lead article on the front page (October 19, 2002) reports on the debate over the so-called zero-tolerance rule adopted by the American Catholic bishops in Dallas. Unfortunately, adopting such a rule is no solution, since the problem begins with the presence of pedophilic priests among the clergy, not their overt behavior. As Cardinal Law of Boston stated (New York Times, April 13, 2002), "In recent years—certainly that would include my tenure as Archbishop—there has been a general recognition that such cases reflect a psychological and emotional pathology." Note his phrase "in recent years." In other words, only recently has the Catholic Church recognized that pedophilia is a psychological disorder. (Child sexual abuse is in addition a serious crime, but the Church has not yet fully recognized that.) The APA Diagnostic and Statistical Manual of mental disorders (DSM-IV) lists pedophilia under the heading of 'paraphilia,' i.e., as a sexual disorder. The zero-tolerance policy should be applied to the disorder, not to acts after they are committed. No person with a pedophilic sexual orientation should ever be allowed to occupy a position of authority over children, period. All efforts, including by the Church, should be directed toward the goal of prevention.

## TO THE EDITOR OF THE NEW YORK TIMES:

## The Rationalization of
## Criminal Child Abuse by Priests

The article in today's Times entitled "1960s Culture Cited as Cause of Priest Abuse (May 18, 2011, p. A1) reports on yet another rationalization of the sex crimes committed by pedophilic priests. In it we read that priests were "poorly monitored, under stress, amid the sexual turmoil of the 1960s." This is no way excuses or even explains why so many priests chose children and adolescents as sex objects, thereby committing heinous crimes that inflicted horrible damage on their victims. Why didn't these men turn to each other for sexual gratification? With readily available partners it would have been convenient, easy to keep quiet and would have caused no scandal. Normal men do not respond sexually to children; they find the idea of sex with children abhorrent and understand also how damaging it would be to the children. I have heard parents say "If anyone tried to have sex with my kids, I'd kill them!" Adults who prey on children in that way are themselves stuck at a stage of psychological development that corresponds roughly to the age of their victims. That's why one priest was quoted in the Times recently as saying that his sex play with a youngster "was all a game." The sexual revolution of the 1960s was about liberating adult sexuality, not condoning child molestation and abuse.

## TO THE EDITOR OF THE NEW YORK TIMES:

## 'Non-Sexual' Sexual Molestation

In "Bishop in Sexual Abuse Case Prompts New Outrage in Belgium" (April 16, 2011, p. A4) Bishop Vangheluwe, who has been accused of sexually molesting his own nephews, described the incidents as follows: "It was a certain intimacy that took place; the nephews slept with me. It began as a game with the boys, and the abuse was restricted to touching of the genitals. They never saw me naked and there was no penetration." The bishop also denied that he was driven by sexual motives, saying "I never felt the slightest sexual attraction." It is entirely possible that he did not feel sexually aroused during the episodes he describes, just as two 10-year-old boys can 'fool around' without experiencing sexual arousal. The behavior he describes is not at all unusual *for preadolescent boys curious to explore their sexuality.* From his own description it is clear that Bishop Vangheluwe is an grown man whose psychosexual and emotional development was arrested and remained that of a preadolescent boy. This is also why he showed so little guilt or contrition about what happened, since he didn't see it as sexual experience at all. I would guess that, like Bishop Vangheluwe, many priests are so sexually inhibited that they really don't feel sexual attraction for anyone, including the children whom they molest. The problem is that they are so naive regarding human sexuality that they are not aware of the damaging effect their inappropriate sexual behavior has on the children. We see something of this blindness also in an entry which Cardinal Law of Boston once made in a priest's record about the priest's known pedophilic activities: "*He fools around with children*"—as if such activities were of no real consequence.

## TO THE EDITOR OF THE NEW YORK TIMES:

## The Latest Priest Listings

In "Archdiocese Of Boston Lists Priests Tied to Abuse" (August 25, 2011, p. A12 ) the Archdiocese of Boston and Cardinal Sean P. O'Malley published a "partial list of clergy members accused of sexual abuse, nearly a decade after a scandal erupted here . . . involving widespread abuse by priests and revelations that the archdiocese had been shielding molesters for years. 132 priests and 2 deacons . . . including priests whom the church or courts have found guilty of sexually abusing a child, others who left the priesthood before or after accusations of abuse, and dead priests who have been publicly accused of abuse." The list includes priests who are on administrative leave while their cases are being investigated. The names of an additional 91 accused diocesan priests were not listed, including 62 dead priests who have not been publicly accused and 22 still alive who could not be proved to have molested children. He decided not to publish a list of names of priests from other religious orders who were accused of sexual abuse while working in the Boston Archdiocese. Victims groups said that there were at least 70 such clergy, including some thought to have had multiple victims. Some called the lists flawed because "they didn't include any names that were not already in the public domain."

Knowing the total number of clergy in the Boston Archdiocese, it would be possible to calculate the percentage that were involved in this sordid 'scandal' over the years. Perhaps that figure will become known some day. In any event, the picture is grim enough that the term scandal is an understatement; it's really a moral disaster for the Catholic Church and an unspeakable tragedy for the thousands of child victims and their families. The hypocrisy of the Catholic Church is obscene: its clergy and leaders freely invoke the name of God to damn those they consider sinners, but they themselves are the ones who belong in Hell.

# Chapter 6

# HOMOSEXUALITY

HOMOSEXUALITY HAS BEEN A PROMINENT topic in the media for quite some time, first in connection with gay rights, then with gays in the military, and then with the gay marriage controversy which is still going on all over the country. Meanwhile, the presence and participation of gays in our society is not new. At the time of the Revolutionary War homosexual activity was a capital crime. It was still illegal in the mid-20th century, when most gays were closeted, gossipy news commentators like Walter Winchell delighted in outing prominent people, and the New York City Police Department's vice squad had *agents provocateurs* who would entrap homosexual men in bars and then arrest them for soliciting sex.

The latter part of the 20th century saw the gay liberation movement and the real beginnings of America's acceptance of homosexuals, including, for instance, the outlawing of job discrimination based on sexual orientation. During the 1980s the AIDS epidemic expanded into a disastrous blight on the gay community, killing thousands before effective prevention and treatment became available. Ronald Reagan, president at that time, was not interested in the issue and did virtually nothing about the devastating epidemic because he and most others considered AIDS a gay men's disease. Only with the massive spread of HIV/AIDS among the general population in Africa was it realized that this was not the case.

Later in the last century the "don't ask, don't tell" was enacted to give homosexuals the privilege and right to serve in the armed forces without discrimination. Now we are seeing movements all over the country to pass laws legalizing gay marriage. The New York State Legislature recently passed the Gay Marriage Bill, the seventh state so far to do so. Each of these issues has been the source of much social, political and religious controversy. The usual tendency to separate church and state doesn't seem to hold in these matters. Although the "don't ask, don't tell" law was repealed by Congress in August 2011, this change has yet to be fully implemented in the armed services.

There are many groups with many opinions regarding homosexuality; this chapter contains my responses to some of the more irrational and objectionable views that have appeared in the media.

The one point raised most frequently and repeated *ad nauseam* by those who argue against homosexuality is the reference to a verse in the Old Testament (Leviticus 20:13) where we find the following one-liner: "Thou shalt not lie with mankind, as with womankind; it is an abomination." Even Senator Jesse Helms used to quote this, full of condemnation, in his booming voice: "It's an abomination!" In fact, the Book of Leviticus, as anyone familiar with the Bible knows, contains a listing of what are now known as the rules of Kosher; according to Leviticus it is also an *abomination* to eat shrimp or to see one's own father or uncle naked. (Some Jews nowadays also consider it an *abomination* to press an elevator button on a Saturday.) The rules were presumably intended to prevent illness (not eating pork to avoid trichinosis, for example) and prohibit work on the Sabbath.

Preachers of many faiths condemn homosexual activity as sinful or unbiblical and point to Leviticus, but they all avoid saying much about adultery and fornication, for if they did they would most likely be preaching to empty pews. According to the New Testament, *all* remarried divorcees are *committing adultery* and *all* extramarital sex is *fornication*. These groups of true sinners, as we know, includes almost the entire population of the United States.

Later on in the section of Leviticus on sexual mores there appears a second lone verse prohibiting homosexuality in the context of strong prohibitions against "uncovering the nakedness" of women other than one's wife and of male relatives such as one's father and uncles.

The prohibition against homosexual acts appears here in an entirely different context along with incest, adultery, fornication and bestiality, all of which are punishable by death or "burning." Leviticus 20:13 says "If a man also lieth with mankind, as he lieth with a woman, both of them have committed an abomination: they shall surely be put to death; their blood shall be upon them." Note, however, that homosexual relations among men are not singled out as being any more sinful than heterosexual sexual activity outside of marriage, all forms of which are likewise punishable by death. A man also may not have sexual relations with any female relative, including mother, sister, aunt, cousin, grandmother, granddaughter and in-laws, under pain of death. And any sexual relations outside of marriage (fornication) are considered a mortal sin.

There are some other interesting transgressions that are associated with rather harsh penalties. "And the daughter of any priest, if she profane herself by playing the whore, she profaneth her father: she shall be burnt with fire." (Leviticus 21:9) It is also interesting to note that there is no mention at all in Leviticus of pedophilia. There is no question that our modern society considers pedophilia far more objectionable than any of the behaviors enumerated above, but apparently the rule makers in biblical times were unconcerned about it. Only recently have churches been forced to turn their attention to this abhorrent phenomenon after centuries of having swept it under the rug and tolerating pedophilia and pedophilic behavior among clergy.

Interestingly, there isn't one word anywhere in the Bible condemning or even mentioning lesbianism. Even today it is largely absent from religious and political discourse on the subject of homosexuality. It is a fact that lesbians are not subject to the disapproval, taunting and violence routinely directed at homosexual men. I suspect there are two reasons for this. On the one hand, the survival of the species depends crucially on propagation through heterosexual mating. Since homosexual men do not participate in this, they are of no use to a society struggling for survival and would naturally be condemned and excluded. Lesbian women, on the other hand, can and do bear children, and therefore do not pose a threat to the survival of the species. Nowadays, lesbians can even have children by arrangement with a male acquaintance or by being artificially inseminated with sperm from an anonymous male. The other, more obvious reason society reserves its strongest prejudices for male homosexuals has to do with the fact that women, except in certain segments of Western society since the mid-20th century, have always been and still are treated as second-class citizens—in all realms of life. That is to say, along with everything else in their lives, women's sexual orientation is of little or no concern to men.

*    *    *

## TO THE EDITOR OF THE NEW YORK TIMES:

The government's recent report on the harassment and mistreatment of gays in the military only shows that these things have not been significantly influenced by White House edicts on the subject. When it comes to homosexuality, our culture is full of misinformation, superstition, misconceptions, phobias and strange attributions of immorality. These attitudes are epitomized by an amusing line in the recent comedy *Analyze This*. Robert De Niro plays a panic-ridden, macho Mafioso type who enters into treatment with a psychiatrist played by the comedian Billy Crystal. One of De Niro's first remarks to his therapist is "If you make a queer out of me, I'll kill you!" In my view, this short line says a lot about the fear of homosexuality which is latent in even the most aggressively masculine of men (it also, incidentally, accurately portrays many people's fear of psychiatrists and misconceptions as to what they can and can't do). The superstitious idea that homosexuality can be somehow taught or caused to appear by suggestion or conscious influence is not uncommon. A patient of mine who had wanted to learn to play the piano when he was young told me his father had refused to get one because he thought it might make his son gay! I also once treated a sailor in the Navy who said other people thought he was gay because he liked the music of Tchaikovsky. The idea expressed by Robert De Niro's character that homosexuality is a possible outcome of psychiatric treatment, though plausible for someone like him and therefore funny, is of course completely absurd.

Former Vice President Dan Quayle once said he firmly believed homosexuals actively choose their lifestyle and sexual orientation. Others on the Christian Right have voiced similar opinions. I call them the Religious Wrong. In fact, this is completely incorrect. There is no scientific evidence indicating that homosexuality is either a voluntary choice by an individual or that it can be caused by a teacher, psychiatrist, Scout Leader, another homosexual or by any other person or relationship, except possibly by early family dysfunction. There are many theories about its cause and no single one of them explains all known instances. The most common psychological 'explanation' for homosexual sexual orientation is fear of heterosexuality. Freud, for his part, thought it was caused by a developmental delay. Other mental health professionals see it simply as another variety of normal human psychosexual development and not a pathological condition at all. In sum, no one has come up with a complete and convincing answer regarding causality and homosexuality.

As for the morality of homosexual behavior, the Bible is frequently and rather bizarrely misapplied to support the conservative religious view of homosexuality as sinful. Homosexual relations between men are mentioned in the Old Testament in the context of a hodgepodge of rules, most of which are aimed at the prevention of disease. The punishments for violating these rules aren't spelled out in detail; rather, there is merely a vague reference to banishment: "For whosoever shall commit any of these abominations, even the souls that commit them shall be cut off from among their people."

Turning to the New Testament, however, we find that the punishments prescribed for *any* form of heterosexual sex outside of marriage are quite severe. As St. Paul writes to the congregation at

Corinth concerning sexuality (I Corinthians, Chapter 7), "It is good for a man not to touch a woman." However, if the alternative would be to fornicate, he says "let every man have his own wife, and let every woman have her own husband." Later on he writes: "For I would that all men were even as I myself," i.e., celibate. Regarding unmarried people and widows he says "It is good for them if they abide even as I. But if they cannot contain [i.e., abstain from sex completely], let them marry: for it is better to marry than to burn."

In other words, according to St. Paul, *all* forms of heterosexual sex outside of marriage are sinful and therefore *prohibited and punishable by burning*. Odd that we don't hear many religious leaders or politicians quoting St. Paul on this point! I suppose that's because if they did, they would stand to lose a lot of parishioners or lose a lot of votes, respectively. (In the opinion of one former Roman Catholic bishop of Newark, N.J., quoted in a recent article in the New York Times, St. Paul was gay.)

A proper understanding of what is going on in the minds of those who harass gay people would help us approach the problem more rationally. There is no doubt that there is an element of homophobia present in those who engage in harassment of gays. The fear that one's own hidden homosexual feelings might surface, as they do frequently in prisons, for instance, is probably one of the factors behind people's hatred toward and persecution of homosexuals. Observers of the prison system have noted that "the only thing prisons cure a man of is his heterosexuality." Another example of a situation in which homosexual activity occurs with regularity among men who are essentially heterosexual is a long tour at sea in the Navy. Don't these facts suggest that that homosexuality is actually *everyone's* second choice? Why is there such a fear and loathing of homosexuality and homosexuals? The fact is, heterosexuals who are not conflicted regarding their own sexuality generally have little or no negative reaction to homosexuality, are comfortable around homosexuals and can relate to them without difficulty. That is, to a psychologically healthy person the sexual orientation of others is of no particular importance. By contrast, people who experience and act on strong negative feelings toward homosexuals are in fact struggling with equally strong forces at work in themselves and desperately fear the possibility that their own unwanted feelings might come to the surface. In other words, the real psychopathology is not homosexuality, but homophobia.

Perhaps there might be less fuss over the subject if it were more widely made known that homosexuality is not a contagious disease, nor is it communicable or even easily brought about in anyone by anyone; that it is not under the control of the individual and is not chosen or wished for; and that, for those who like to moralize about sexuality, there is no biblical basis to consider it more morally wrong than any other sexual orientation. Furthermore, if straight men and women would get over their fear that they might have homosexual urges in themselves, they would no longer fear homosexuals or feel the need to persecute them.

## TO THE EDITOR OF THE NEW YORK TIMES:

## The Religious Wrong

A recent article in the Times told of a plan by the Southern Baptist Convention to boycott some Disney Corp. productions in protest against Disney's apparent sympathy for homosexuals and their lifestyle. The group seemed particularly bothered by the hosting of a television program by Ellen DeGeneres, who is openly gay, and the company's job benefits for employees who are in gay couples. The Baptists justify their anti-gay attitude by quoting the usual verse from Leviticus. The Book of Leviticus, it must be said, is not high on the reading list in most Christian congregations, nor does it in other respects have much impact on the behavior and lives of Christians. Leviticus merely reflects the fact that early priests apparently were aware of infectious diseases and devised complicated rules prohibiting the eating of certain 'unclean' animals and requiring that people suffering from infectious diseases be isolated to protect the populace from contagion. The rules concerning animals may also have derived from ancient animal-related superstitions.

Leviticus lists in detail the animals which it is forbidden to eat and describes complicated dietary rules, some of which have survived to this day and are part of what are now called the rules of Kosher. According to Leviticus, one must not eat rabbits, camels, any shell fish, eagles, ospreys, vultures, ravens, hawks, owls, swans, weasels, mice, tortoises, chameleons, lizards or snails—just to name a few. Leviticus describes the eating of any of these animals as an 'abomination.' (Interestingly, it's perfectly fine to eat such things as locusts, beetles and grasshoppers. Nice diet, eh?) The term 'abomination' as used in Leviticus seems to refer to that which is unclean and should therefore be avoided for health reasons. For instance, we know that the prohibition against eating pork, observed in some religions to this day, is directly related to the spread of trichinosis.

In a similar vein, there is a rule in Leviticus prohibiting homosexuality, intended presumably to prevent the spread of sexually transmitted diseases. This would have been a wise rule indeed, since at that time, and throughout history prior to the introduction of antibiotics in the 1930s and 40s, besides the familiar syphilis and gonorrhea there were plenty of other nasty sexually transmitted diseases one never hears about any more because they have been virtually eradicated.

I wonder what the reaction would be if the Southern Baptist Convention were to attempt to prohibit *all* the behaviors referred to as 'abominations' in Leviticus with the same fervor it reserves for homosexuality? It would mean, for one, that they, the Southern Baptists, would all need to be strictly Kosher in their daily lives. It would also mean they would need to speak out forcefully against the 'abomination' of fornication, which is to say *any form of sex outside of marriage*. This would be quite a public relations challenge, since, as we know, our culture is quite an unapologetically fornicating one. Our literature, theater, movies and television programming is jam-packed with all sorts of behavior that comes under the definition of fornication. We know that our adolescents are busy fornicating like crazy and no one even tries to stop them. Condoms are being distributed in our schools! In fact, far from being seen as a behavior that has to be stopped, fornication has become so widespread that it now appears to be considered normal. Even the churches, apparently, have decided that to try to change this is futile.

In fact, to be at all consistent with their professed reliance on Leviticus and the rest of the Bible for moral guidance, Southern Baptists should be boycotting just about every form of cultural activity taking place outside of churches and their own homes, including much of what is happening in the public schools—virtually everything, that is, except perhaps classical music and hymn-singing.

And that would be just the tip of the iceberg. One often hears the argument that homosexuality is a threat to family values. What about the threat to family values posed by the staggering rate of divorce, teenage pregnancy and out-of-wedlock births? You'd think the Southern Baptists would be so busy railing against the 'abominations' being committed by heterosexual Americans on a mass scale and glorified in their entertainment that they'd hardly have time to concern themselves with a few homosexuals.

## TO THE EDITOR OF THE RECORD:

## The Crucial Question of Same-Sex Marriage

The ongoing controversy over the morality of gay relationships and the legality of gay marriages cannot be brought to a fair and rational resolution until a very basic question is finally and unequivocally answered: Is homosexuality inborn (and therefore, for the religious, God-given) or is it a matter of individual choice? Given that our society, despite all that has changed, still disapproves of everything gay, it seems obvious that no one would voluntarily *choose* to be gay even if that were possible (which most experts agree it clearly isn't). Given the American Psychiatric Association's delisting of homosexuality as a pathological condition and the total lack of clinical evidence that it can be 'cured,' experts are now overwhelmingly of the opinion that homosexuality is either innate or else is determined very early in one's development and is therefore essentially normal for those individuals. It is therefore incumbent upon society to treat them as such.

## TO THE EDITOR OF THE NEW YORK TIMES: JUNE 30, 2003

### Getting It Straight on Homosexuality

Implicit in the public discourse of our religious and political leaders on the legal and moral issues surrounding homosexuality is the idea that homosexuality can be seen as the hedonistic, immoral, antisocial and even criminal behavior of essentially normal people who have chosen it as an alternative life-style.

Then they trot out the Old Testament, in which homosexuality is referred to as 'an abomination'—along with a long list of other behaviors that people nowadays engage in all the time, such as eating shrimp and a whole list of other foods. Speaking of biblical prohibitions on sex, the New Testament actually spends much more time condemning and prohibiting *all* forms of sex outside of marriage by anyone, anywhere—the biblical term is 'fornication'—than it does forbidding homosexuality. Were our political and religious leaders to start quoting the biblical passages forbidding all forms of unmarried sex, they would be voted out of office and out of their pulpits—perhaps actually laughed out—and they know it!

There was a time when many homosexuals sought treatment to 'cure' or change their sexual orientation, but ever since the increased cultural acceptance of homosexuality this is no longer common. Since the American Psychiatric Association removed homosexuality from the Diagnostic and Statistical Manual as a disorder with a psychiatric diagnosis, one of the effects has been to drastically lower the suicide rate in gays who, in former times, couldn't deal with the condemnation of their families, society in general and religious dogma in particular. (One does still occasionally read of such unfortunate occurrences.)

Until our political and religious leaders and society in general get it straight about homosexuality, there is little chance that decisions made regarding the legality and morality of homosexuality will be even remotely reasonable, rational or fair to this group of our fellow citizens.

Mr. Ralph Reed
Century Strategies
3235 Satellite Blvd
Duluth, GA 30096
June 2, 1998

Dear Mr. Reed:

I watched your interview with Larry King last evening and am appalled at your abysmal ignorance of the facts of human psychosexual development. You're obviously an intelligent man, but your espousal of the view that homosexuality is the result of a voluntary choice is absurd and reveals that your bigotry, masquerading as religious belief, has completely blinded you and prevents you from having a rational understanding of a phenomenon that has been the subject of considerable scientific study. There is a significant literature on the subject of homosexuality and nowhere will you find anyone who even suggests that the choice of sexual orientation can in any way be influenced by a conscious, voluntary decision. No one can just *choose* to be sexually aroused by a person of the same sex.

That people would voluntarily choose a sexual identity for which they know society will mock, condemn, harass and even perhaps kill them, is incomprehensible. Why do you suppose the suicide rate among homosexuals is so much higher than in the general public? The intense self-loathing and consequent depression experienced by many homosexuals because of their sexual orientation is well known and difficult to address therapeutically. If it is their choice and so marvelous, why the depression and suicide? People who express views like yours on this subject only cause more pain and distress.

No one has a complete understanding of the phenomenon of homosexuality, though it appears to depend to some extent on setting and individual psychological makeup. What is known is that it has a large genetic component and may also be influenced by family and early psychological development. Just what it is that finally determines homosexual orientation is not entirely clear, but we do know that it occurs very early in life, much earlier than the age of reason and therefore much earlier than an individual could conceivably make such a decision consciously.

Equally obvious is that the whole business of expressing hostile attitudes toward homosexuality is a politically calculated move on your part aimed at attracting other ignorant bigots, which is unfortunate.

By the way, are you aware that men who experience the strongest aversion to gays are usually trying to deny their own leanings in this direction? Gay-bashers are in effect saying to the world, "I have no homosexual feelings. I hate these people." In fact, what they hate are their own latent homosexual feelings and so they desperately try to reassure themselves that they are 100 percent straight. Psychologically healthy men, meanwhile, have little or no reaction to gays. The ones who so loudly proclaim their disgust at homosexuality are revealing what we call a reaction-formation against their own homosexual stirrings. It's called homophobia.

Rather than continuing to make an utter fool of yourself by expressing harmful views on a subject about which you very obviously know nothing, why don't you read some of the extensive medical and psychological literature on the subject? Educate yourself on the subject before you show your ignorance any further, Mr. Reed.

(Ralph Reed is a prominent ultra-conservative religious leader and spokesperson.)

ALEX CAEMMERER JR. M.D.

## TO THE EDITOR OF THE NEW YORK TIMES:

As reported in the Times recently, a momentous meeting that the Reverend Jimmy Falwell held with 200 pro-gay clergymen attracted a large contingent of anti-gay demonstrators who objected, ironically, to what they viewed as Falwell's excessive tolerance as seen in his willingness to have a dialog. In response he had to reiterate and emphasize his well-known opinion that the Bible views homosexuality as a sin.

To single out homosexuality as particularly sinful, even in biblical terms, is selective and discriminatory and ignores the fact that the New Testament contains strong prohibitions against other kinds of sexual behavior, including heterosexual behavior, and in particular against *all sex of any kind outside of marriage*. The prohibitions against the latter are strong and carry the threat of severe punishment. St. Paul, for instance, in his letter to the Corinthians (1 Cor. 7:1-9) states "It is good for a man not to touch a woman. Nevertheless, to avoid fornication, let every man have his own wife, and let every woman have her own husband . . . For I would that all men were even as myself [i.e., celibate] . . . I say therefore to the unmarried and widows, It is good for them if they abide even as I. But if they cannot contain, let them marry: for it is better to marry than to burn."

That is, according to the Bible, extramarital *heterosexual* sex is a much more serious sin than homosexual sex and is to be punished severely, namely through burning in Hell! None of the numerous 'abominations' listed in Leviticus, including homosexual relations, appears to lead to such dire consequences.

I have never heard any of our conservative religious and political leaders—the ones who quote scripture to assail homosexuality—cite any of these clear statements in the Bible condemning heterosexual activity. Were they to do so, my guess is that their popularity would plummet precipitously.

## TO THE EDITOR OF THE NEW YORK TIMES:

In "The Homosexual Exception" (February 7, 1998, Magazine) Alan Wolfe poses the question as to why homosexuals and lesbians are the only groups that still experience prejudice and nonacceptance by the majority of our society.

In my view, the answer may not lie in the realm of moral judgments at all, but rather in biology. The primary goal of human society is to perpetuate itself, and most human behavior is aimed at assuring this goal. One of the likely reasons that most societies traditionally condemn homosexual behavior is that it doesn't contribute to the propagation of the species. Any factor that has a negative impact on reproduction is vigorously condemned out of a biological imperative. Up until fairly recently the survival of the species has been tenuous, at best, and humankind has needed all the reproducers possible in order to survive in a world filled with deadly, incurable endemic diseases of all kinds punctuated by epidemics like the bubonic plague that decimated Europe in the Middle Ages.

My own grandmother, born in this county in 1865, was one of two out of 11 siblings to survive to adulthood. Whole families used to be wiped out by contagious diseases. It was only in the 1930s that antibiotics finally became available and doctors could cure some illnesses that previously had had very high mortality rates.

Life expectancy in the US is now well into the seventies and rising and we no longer need everyone to have a lot of babies. In the 1930s the population of the US was 125 million; it is now over 300 million. At this rate, it will double within the lifetime of the current generation of young people.

China has already taken steps to address the problem of overpopulation. Unfortunately, since by law a couple can't have more than one child and Chinese prefer male offspring, female babies are not infrequently left to die or else offered up for adoption by foreigners. (This has recently become illegal.) One can imagine the outrage if this were to occur in the United States. At the present rate of population growth, however, we will be in the same situation as China in the not too distant future, so it would actually be to our great advantage to lower the birth rate. In any case, it is clear that homosexual behavior is no longer an impediment to the survival of the species and so there is no longer a biological imperative to discourage it.

Neither is there any particular reason to consider homosexual behavior any more or less moral than heterosexual behavior, not even if one looks to the Bible for guidance. The Bible actually has some very strict things to say about heterosexual sex, for instance, that *any* sex with a person who has been divorced (including within a second marriage) is 'adultery' and *any* form of sex outside of marriage is 'fornication.' Our culture has virtually ignored these passages, no doubt because to take them seriously one would be forced to admit that we are a land of adulterers and fornicators.

## Evangelists and Homosexuality

Evangelical religious perceptions and attitudes towards homosexuality have been limited to the question of its morality. Few have made the attempt to address its causes and whether the condition can be altered by any sort of intervention. These religious leaders rarely speak of, let alone sermonize or moralize about *heterosexual sex*, about which the New Testament has plenty to say. Jesus himself in three different places states unambiguously that any time a divorced person remarries, the relationship is *adulterous*. And adultery is one of the Ten Commandments! It is likely that if churches were to address this subject with congregations, membership would dwindle to a very inhibited few. (Apparently the divorce rate in the so-called Bible states is even higher than in the so-called secular states.)

The subject of homosexuality is a complicated one, and there are no definitive answers yet as to its causes and origins. Most expert opinion favors the idea of inheritance or prenatal influences. Certainly there seems to be a genetic predisposition which might then be intensified by a delay in sexual maturation. One recent study indicated that as the number of males born in a family increases, so does the probability that the youngest one will be gay.

What is clear is that no one can consciously choose their sexual orientation. If that were possible, homosexual people who are extremely unhappy with their sexual orientation, even to the point of considering suicide, would simply change their orientation. Nor do any studies indicate that homosexuality can be changed or 'cured' by any sort of psychological or pharmacological intervention. One of the more tolerant religious leaders once commented that if it were ever shown that homosexuality was genetic rather than a matter of choice, i.e., predetermined and not amenable to change, "then we would have to think again about its morality."

Bill O'Reilly
Fox News

Dear Mr. O'Reilly,

On this evening's program you discussed the arrest of some gay men for allegedly engaging in sex in public. You called them "perverts" and their behavior "immoral."

Well, Bill, have you read the Bible lately? The Bible addresses homosexuality in the Old Testament Book of Leviticus, in which "mankind sleeping with mankind" is called an "abomination." Reading a little further, we note that, according to Leviticus, it's also an "abomination" to eat shrimp, or to see your father or uncle naked, or to wear clothes with both linen and wool in the same garment. Pretty shocking, eh Bill? Do your eat shrimp, Bill?

As I'm sure you know, in the New Testament Jesus himself says "Whosoever shall put away his wife [i.e., divorce her], except for fornication, and shall marry another, committeth adultery; and whoso marrieth her which is put away doth commit adultery." Other than this, Jesus never said anything about sexual mores.

However, St. Paul (whom even some priests believe was gay) did have plenty to say about 'fornication,' by which he meant any sexual behavior outside of marriage by anyone anywhere, saying that he would prefer that everyone were as he, namely, celibate. But that "if one cannot contain" [i.e., abstain from sex] one should get married, for "it is better to marry than to burn."

So when are you going to tell all the divorcees and re-married people and all the unmarried sexually active people, from teenagers to lonely senior citizens in nursing homes, that they are immoral, are living in sin and are going to burn for it? When are you going to start campaigning for strict laws outlawing divorce and making all sex outside of marriage illegal? Perhaps you've accepted the fact, Bill, that ours is a country of adulterers and fornicators. But why then do you single out the sexual behavior of homosexuals?

By the way, Bill, your use of the term "pervert" is inappropriate, inaccurate and reveals your ignorance on the subject. The medical term for abnormal sexuality is "paraphilia" and it is not applied to homosexuality. Homosexuality occurs in all cultures and at all times in about the same percentage of the population. The cause of homosexuality is not fully understood, but it seems most likely to be either inherited, i.e., genetic, or else determined very early in human development, possibly in the womb. It is in no way anyone's conscious choice, though this is a very widespread opinion held by people who are totally ignorant on the subject. Many have expressed that opinion, including that brilliant thinker, former Vice President Dan Quayle. But if you think about it, who would ever consciously choose to be the object of society's revulsion?

You seem to be quite intelligent, Bill, so why don't you educate yourself on the subject of human sexuality and cut out the ignorant moralizing?

# Chapter 7

## VIOLENCE

VIOLENCE IS A PERENNIAL THEME in the American media. Acts of terrorism are becoming increasingly common throughout the world, but the most troubling form of violence is that which occurs among young people in our own country—high school students who get a hold of weapons and go on homicidal rampages the likes of which never used to occur here. Not infrequently, the perpetrators are socially inept young men who were bullied or otherwise excluded from the everyday activities of the majority and who seem to be taking their frustration and anger out on the successful students. It is an urgent problem that requires effective measures to avert further tragedies.

\*   \*   \*

# TO THE EDITOR OF THE NEW YORK TIMES: DECEMBER 12, 1997

## The Tragedy at Paducah High School in Kentucky

The recent tragedy in Paducah High School in Kentucky is not surprising in view of the changes that have taken place in our culture over the years.

We all experience destructive thoughts, wishes and impulses at times, including death wishes and murderous fantasies. Most of these remain unconscious, sometimes manifesting as obsessions or phobias or appearing in dreams, but they can also appear more overtly, for example under the influence of alcohol or drugs.

Most of us are able to control our inappropriate impulses. Fear of punishment is also a deterrent—if there were suddenly no more police or prisons, the murder rate would no doubt skyrocket. However, society relies mostly on our individual consciences to keep the peace. (In recent years, some prominent athletes have turned out to be poor role models for impulse control. This is to some extent understandable, since they are coached to be as aggressive as possible, and hence exercising restraint and impulse control is harder for them.)

Ours is a violent and in some ways cruel society. It is contemptuous of those it perceives as failures: the weak, the ineffective, homosexuals, persons with darker skin, the mentally ill—anyone the majority perceives as being different from itself and therefore abnormal. These are society's rejects. The majority, meanwhile, glorifies the rich and famous, the strong and aggressive, and the bone-breaking athletes.

We love guns. Our movies and TV shows overflow with graphic, revoltingly gory scenes of murder—individual and mass—committed either with hair-raising indifference or unbridled enthusiasm for the sheer thrill and delight of viewers. Depictions of random killings have become part of our daily entertainment. We can thank the modern interpretation of the First Amendment for this boon. (There was a time not so long ago when a movie could not be shown in theaters in this country if it depicted a crime that went unpunished! Another amusing example of how standards of acceptable behavior have changed is the recent announcement that the "F-word" may henceforth be used freely in print or broadcast media—but only as an adjective, not as a verb!)

When vulnerable individuals experience repeated rejection, disappointment and failure it can build up inside them as rage. When this rage combines with intense feelings of hopelessness and an essentially suicidal indifference to consequences, the result is extremely dangerous. This combination is frequently present at least in some measure in people who commit acts of violence. Once a person adopts the attitude of "I don't care what happens to me—after all, no one else does" they feel free to do anything they happen to feel like doing.

With the ubiquitous presence of violence in our society, the availability of lethal weapons and the increasing relaxation of rules and laws against impulsive behavior in recent decades, it is not surprising that controls fail in the unstable and disenfranchised. That is not to say that these factors are the cause of violent behavior; but they do seem to lower the barriers to actions which were once essentially unheard of. Certainly we should not be surprised that violence is now as prevalent as it is. Our newfound freedoms have been costly: random killing has become part of our culture.

## TO THE EDITOR OF THE NEW YORK TIMES:

## The High School Shooting in Littleton, Colorado

The recent shooting at a high school in Colorado, the latest in a growing list of such disquieting events, has given rise, as usual, to any number of attempts by experts and authorities to explain this contemporary American phenomenon. What is obvious is that the perpetrators of such events are young people with severe disturbances, the exact nature of which has still not been understood or adequately explained by anyone. In my opinion, they are the fallout of changes which have taken place in our society—the result of not one but a number of factors operating in contemporary America. Unusual behavior is usually determined by multiple factors and is an expression of a confluence if inner and outer stimuli, the force of which overpowers an individual's ability to control his or her impulses. I would like to suggest a few of the societal factors that may be contributing to the development of the disturbances seen in these teenagers. To me they appear to be a consequence of the changes which have taken place in our society as a whole.

No doubt these young people could be classified as having a mental disorder, since underlying their behavior are overpowering rage, poor impulse control and violent self-destructive and outwardly destructive impulses. They also appear to be alienated from society, to the extent that they show total disregard for societal approval and human life. In addition to being violent, they also appear to be suicidally depressed.

The recent suicide of an unusually attractive star athlete and honor student in an affluent town in Connecticut was just as shocking as the homicides in the schools in Colorado, and equally incomprehensible. Was this an example of what is known as suicide by police action, in which a person purposefully engages in violent behavior with the intention of being killed by a policeman? The dynamics at work in the Colorado and Connecticut cases may have been quite similar; both forms of behavior are signs of severe depression.

Depression is perhaps the most underdiagnosed condition in our society. Most doctors are not adequately trained to detect it in its early stages, most families try to deny its existence and most of those suffering from it, especially males, resist the idea of seeking help or treatment.

There are several contemporary cultural phenomena which might be contributing to the development of the other disorders we see in these very disturbed individuals.

Recent years have seen an increasing awareness of ADHD (Attention Deficit Hyperactivity Disorder) in children and more frequent diagnoses of the disorder, which has approached epidemic proportions. Prescriptions for Ritalin and Prozac to treat this condition have skyrocketed. (In my view, it is sad but true that Ritalin and Prozac are the new mothers of America.) A child psychiatrist colleague of mine, complaining that children's lives these days center around things instead of people, told me "You don't see many mothers in the waiting room with their children any more" i.e., it is the nannies who bring them. The question is, do these children really have ADHD, or is their restlessness, agitation, irritability and anger an expression of their unmet need for attention, nurturing and parental support? In my view, they are suffering from a depressive disorder.

Another psychiatric condition which is being diagnosed more and more frequently is borderline personality disorder. A person with this condition has an emotional makeup heavily dominated by anger, almost to the exclusion of all other emotions, and has great difficulty making and sustaining normal interpersonal relationships. Those suffering from it are often self-destructive and given to impulsive and violent acting out. It has been shown that it is often the result of early emotional deprivation, and signs of the disorder usually also appear quite early in life. A number of years ago I asked an expert on this disorder his opinion as to its causes. He told me that most of his cases were from two-career families.

One hears now of mothers who are so involved in their demanding careers that they turn their newborns over to nannies six weeks after delivery and go back to jobs that keep them away from home from breakfast to dinnertime. How much energy and interest can a woman in a demanding career offer an infant after a hard day at the office? What is the effect of insufficient mothering in early infancy? Dr. Brazelton, the well-known Boston pediatrician, has impressively demonstrated that early bonding between mothers and newborns is critical and should take place during at least the first 6 months of life and ideally much longer. Early emotional deprivation has been strongly implicated in such disorders as borderline personality disorder and depression.

The women's liberation movement of recent decades has certainly changed the role of women in our society and has therefore also had an impact on child-rearing practices. Much has been gained for women, who can now find fulfillment and satisfaction in many areas previously closed to them. It has taken some economic pressure off men and added much to the lives of women. For the women who want to "have it all," however, it has not been that rosy. All too often men have not been willing to step in and take some of the burden of homemaking off the shoulders of their working wives.

Early on, activists in the women's movement promoted the idea that a healthy, self-respecting woman would naturally feel unfulfilled by being nothing more (!) than a homemaker and mother. This prompted many women who perhaps actually would have wanted to stay at home to go ahead and develop careers and spend more time out of the home. As women's careers became more important and demanding and stimulating, the prospect of a life of nothing but homemaking and child rearing no doubt did appear dull to some. Thus, women who "wanted it all" tried to do both. Children may be suffering as a result. Are ADHD, depressive disorders and other emotional problems in children related to these changes?

As for external stimuli in our culture that may be contributing to the violent acting out of impulses by vulnerable teenagers, the media stand out as one culprit. *The Matrix*, a recent and wildly popular movie, is a good example of what our children and teenagers are exposed to. Aside from stunning special effects, it treats the audience to a truly extraordinary amount of gratuitous, ear-splitting, wildly violent, random automatic rifle fire that goes on interminably and for no specific reason or purpose. What effect do these sorts of stimuli have on teenagers who are feeling weak, ineffective and inadequate?

In response to the recent incident in Littleton, Colorado, we hear commentators wondering how this could happen in such a quiet, middle-class community with its family and religious values and suggesting that this was something you might expect to see happen in a place like New York City. Hold on just a minute! Let's look at how these two communities actually differ. Small-town America values conformity, conventional behavior and traditional activities and is profoundly intolerant of all that is different. Atheism is a bad word in small-town America. Atheists, gays, lesbians, and 'nerds,' to name a few, are not welcome there. New York City, meanwhile, for all its problems, is actually far more tolerant of people who are different or unconventional. It's far easier to do your own thing in New York City without attracting attention, rejection and animosity.

In much of small-town America, football is the second, if not first, religion. A teenage boy had better be an athlete and go to church like everyone else, or he will be "out," ridiculed, despised and probably excluded socially. He had certainly better not come out if he is gay. What effect do these pressures have on young people with shaky self-images, self-doubts or histories of failure? Could they contribute to the rage and alienation characteristic of the desperate young people who lash out in these violent school episodes?

We all like winners. In the all-American, competitive striving for social popularity, occupational achievement, athletic superiority, affluence and the good life, the ones who are less fortunate—the losers—are viewed with contempt and either ignored or actively made to feel like failures. For a young person who does not have that feeling of security which a child develops early in life from a strong, loving family, this can easily stoke feelings of self-loathing, frustration, hopelessness and rage.

I am by no means suggesting that these factors entirely explain why horribly violent outbursts have become regular occurrences in our schools. But certainly we can say that these events are a consequence of our modern culture, even if we don't know which specific elements of it are at work. They can't be seen as isolated instances of bizarre behavior by a few bad apples. We as a society had better examine ourselves and learn what we are doing wrong. Whether it's our child-rearing practices, our attitudes towards the 'losers' and less fortunate among us or our inattention to psychological stressors and rejection of help and treatment for emotional disorders, the problem appears to be related to basic attitudes in our rapidly changing culture.

# TO THE EDITOR OF THE NEW YORK TIMES:

## High School Shootings

The question as to the cause of the recent tragic school killings is less compelling to me than the question as to why these events are such a surprise to so many people. In my view, profound cultural changes that have occurred in our society over the last three decades are largely responsible for what is happening. Women have shifted their attention and energy from child rearing to careers. Infants are routinely given to caretakers when they are only 6 weeks old. A divorce used to be a disgrace and difficult to obtain (and these were also not such good things), but with the advent of easy divorce many families have given way to one-parental households. Hence the schools now find themselves *in loco parentis*, a position they are neither equipped nor willing to assume. In earlier times one would be sent home for saying the word 'condom' in school; nowadays teachers pass them out in class! Spit balls used to be the ammunition of choice in our schools; now it is bullets fired from automatic weapons!

The sexual revolution (the dumbest idea of the century, in my opinion) has lifted both internal and external restraints on sexual behavior. The corollary to this change in our national character has been a similar weakening of restraints on aggressive behavior. These two areas of human behavior are psychologically related and often parallel each other. The disinhibiting effect spreads from one to the other. We now have the newly observed phenomena of 'date rape' and 'road rage'—good examples of the failure of inner behavioral controls. We've truly opened wide Pandora's legendary box.

TV, movies and other media have responded to these newfound freedoms (and consumer interest and demands) and compete with each other to see how far they can go, challenging societal mores at every chance. (The media usually win.) Sex and violence are popular, profitable and ubiquitous in our modern society.

In addition, the widespread availability of guns and the escalation of their potency in the form of automatic weapons such as the Glock have made the acting out of unrestrained impulses deadly. We have seen what happens when individuals with emotional instability and poor impulse control have ready access to these weapons. As they go through adolescence young people experience increasingly intense impulses, both sexual and aggressive, but their inner behavioral controls remain immature.

Cultural mores, religious institutions and parental supervision have all lost the ability to resist the general relaxation of what is considered acceptable behavior.

It would seem that the extreme violence taking place in our schools is a natural consequence of the major cultural changes in our society in these last decades, and should therefore come as no surprise. What is surprising is that as our cultural mores and behavior controls were actively and purposefully modified, if not eliminated entirely, the possible consequences were not considered seriously, if at all. This is often the case with revolutionary ideas. Unfortunately, Pandora's box, once opened, is not easily closed.

## TO THE EDITOR OF THE NEW YORK TIMES:

## The Sopranos

Having been caught up myself in the fascination with the TV series *The Sopranos*, I have wondered about the reasons for its widespread appeal. On the surface, the answer is the outstanding quality of the writing, acting and production. All the characterizations are beautifully conceived and true to life. One forgets this is theater and views the experience as real. However, as a psychiatrist I am also interested in the unconscious reasons for its success.

The show centers around unusual amounts of violence and other unsavory behavior in the lives of otherwise more or less ordinary people living in the suburbs of New Jersey. In my opinion, the appeal of this program is its portrayal of impulses which are present in all of us but which are repressed to varying degrees and never reach consciousness. Watching the Sopranos allows us to vicariously have the thoughts and do the things the characters do without being punished or feeling guilty. Tellingly, the show's characters, except for Carmela, don't show many signs of guilt. In real life, the only thing that keeps people from all sorts of mean, criminal, and even murderous behavior is the fear of punishment, either by one's own conscience or the criminal justice system. Imagine what our society would be like if there were no police around?

This is what theater is all about: allowing us to identify with and vicariously behave as the characters do without feeling guilty or being punished. It's kind of comforting now and then to see such familiar, everyday people be so absolutely rotten.


## TO THE EDITOR OF THE NEW YORK TIMES: NOVEMBER 7, 2009


### Isn't It Obvious It Was a Suicide Bombing? And, He Was No Psychiatrist

In the article "Little Evidence of Terror Plot in Fort Hood Base Killings" (November 8, 2009, p. 1) we read that "investigators have not ruled out the possibility that Major Hasan believed he was carrying out an extremist suicide mission." Are they kidding? Isn't that obviously exactly what it was? (31 soldiers were massacred.) A man attacks and kills military personnel while obviously expecting to be killed himself—what else would you call it? He was known to have spoken in favor of suicide bombings and to have once declared that if he were deployed to Iraq or Afghanistan he would not participate in the killing of Muslims, presumably including enemy Muslims. Apparently his views on suicide bombings had been known for years! It seems quite clear to me that he simply switched sides in the wars in the Middle East and decided to kill

American troops by going on a shooting spree which he must have known would end in his death.

Which segues into the next obvious conclusion: this man was no psychiatrist! He may have studied psychiatry, but anyone who supports suicide bombings of innocent civilians doesn't have the moral qualifications to be a physician, whose basic goals are healing and the preservation of life, and shouldn't be practicing medicine. He is a disgrace to the profession of psychiatry and it is an insult to the profession to continue to associated his name with it.

Some have voiced the opinion that one would have to be mentally ill to do such a thing. But for many in the Middle East, suicide bombings are an acceptable and laudable sacrifice for God and country. One high-ranking Palestinian politician, a mother, reportedly said that she was proud of her son who gave his life as a suicide bomber and that if she had 100 more sons she would gladly sacrifice them for the same cause. Any questions?

Bill O'Reilly
Fox News

Dear 'Doctor' O'Reilly:

Speaking on your program the other night about the Fort Hood attack, you stated that the shooter had suddenly "cracked" under the strain and that this accounted for his violent attack on the soldiers. You concluded, on the basis of your vast experience as a psychiatrist, that his behavior represented the sudden onset of a serious psychiatric disorder. Other 'experts' have diagnosed post-traumatic stress disorder. Well, I have been practicing psychiatry for a few decades, and this man's behavior strikes me as being that of an Islamic extremist, not someone who is mentally ill. He had purchased an automatic weapon months before, was known to have approved of suicide bombings, was known to have had stated that he would not participate in the killing of any Muslims and that he approved of Muslim resistance to America's making war on them in the Middle East. It seems obvious to me that he simply changed sides in the war on terrorism. What he did was the equivalent of a suicide bombing. Is it your view that that all suicide bombers are mentally ill? What about the high ranking Palestinian official, a mother, who went on record saying she was proud of her suicide-bomber son, and that if she had 100 more sons she would gladly sacrifice them too as suicide bombers. Is this mental illness? Or is it extremist, fanatical religion? Extremist organizations have warned us that they have plans to commit further attacks abroad, so don't be surprised if that happens. Their 'craziness' is that they genuinely believe that suicide bombers go to heaven and have 70 virgins at their disposal as a reward! That, I will agree, does sound crazy or, in psychiatric terms, delusional. Unfortunately, many religious beliefs are delusions; but when they are shared and accepted by large numbers of people, for instance by members of the religion in question, they are no longer considered symptoms of mental illness.

# Chapter 8

# MISCELLANEOUS

## The Money Addicts

AT A RECENT COLUMBIA UNIVERSITY graduation the graduates from each school were introduced in turn by the Chancellor of the university. When it was the turn of the MBAs to be introduced, they threw showers of fake money in the air, cheering. Most of them are headed for Wall Street or businesses connected with Wall Street, and the gesture was very revealing of their mentality: they are the next generation of players in the Big Money Game, the biggest game around. The game is also called Chasing the Buck and is played in three big arenas on Wall Street known as the New York Stock Exchange, the Nasdaq and the Amex. The score is tallied in dollars and players in this league are ranked by net worth, the sum of their financial assets. This wealth is typically used to acquire trophies, such as Manhattan penthouses or colossal luxury apartments elsewhere decorated by top decorators, luxury cars, million—or multi-million-dollar yachts, impressionist paintings and, of course, palatial waterfront summer homes in the Cash Hamptons or, even more upscale, in Palm Beach, better known as Obscene Beach, where a large number of the super-rich congregate, perhaps to be near our most illustrious trophy seeker, Donald Trump and his Mar-a-Largo Club. There are some who feel that until you are ensconced in some expensive piece of real estate in Palm Beach, you haven't really arrived.

The Donald is our biggest phallocentric collector of blonds since John F. Kennedy. Kennedy's big ego trip was shooting the moon, whereas the Donald gets his kicks erecting phallic real estate monuments to himself. His next project is to build the tallest building in the world in Chicago to outdo the current record holder in Sri Lanka.

Any self-respecting player has a private Learjet, of course, but even these expensive toys are no longer considered very impressive: the ultimate is now to own a Boeing. I wonder what will happen when there are so many super-rich that these personal flying behemoths start to overcrowd airports? Maybe the next transportation trophy for the really big players will be a $20,000,000 Tito-style daytrip into outer space.

In some Wall Street circles, expensive mistresses are apparently traded in much the same way as stocks. These dolls tend to require luxury apartments, lavish clothes, cars and jewels and have been known to switch from one 'sponsor' to another depending on the perks offered.

The odd thing about all of this is that no one in this hyper-successful group ever seems to be *satisfied*, even with all this wealth. (One exception is Warren Buffet, who says no one needs more than $250,000 a year to live on and brags that he sleeps on the same brand of mattress as everyone else, buys his suits off the rack and lives in a house he bought ages ago for $40,000.) Instead, the super-rich are in a constant state of *tumescence* (arousal and enlargement), perpetually desirous of more and larger ego trips, never able to achieve the release of *detumescence* and, with it, satisfaction and contentment. I recall a patient who once came to me for psychiatric treatment because, as he put it, "I can't be satisfied. When I had one million, I needed five. When I got the five, I needed ten. Now that I have the ten, I need twenty. I never feel as if I've accomplished *anything at all*, much less achieved success."

A similar compulsion may have been driving the billionaire owner of one of the more prominent and successful hedge funds who was convicted of insider trading and sentenced to 11 years in prison and a $10,000,000 fine. He was quoted as saying "I have to win." (This is not the only highly successful hedge fund manager to self-destruct in this manner.)

One sad footnote to the recent Enron debacle was the suicide of one of the company's top executives. He already had a mansion and a 72-foot yacht, but before his death he had planned to trade the yacht in for a larger and faster one. Poor guy.

There have been stories in the press recently suggesting that some prominent Wall Street analysts are not entirely objective in their pronouncements. This is supposed to be news? The Enron crash has probably caused more damage to the economy than the attacks on 9/11. These are just a few examples of the enormous price we all pay for the recklessness of the money addicts.

## TO THE EDITOR OF THE NEW YORK TIMES: JULY 2001

### The Public Legal System

The first paragraph of an article in today's Times reads "Dozens of inmates on death row lack lawyers for their appeals in part because private law firms are increasingly unwilling to take on burdensome, expensive and emotionally wrenching capital cases, death penalty lawyers say."

What if we rewrite this paragraph as follows: "Dozens of seriously ill patients lack doctors and nurses for their treatment, in part because doctors and hospitals are increasingly unwilling to take on burdensome, expensive (owing to wrongful death suits) and emotionally wrenching cases where the patient's life is at stake, malpractice lawyers say."

Later in the article, Sandra Day O'Connor comments, "One troubling feature of the capital punishment system" is that it "may well be allowing some innocent defendants to be executed." Again, rewritten that would read "One troubling feature of the health care system is that it may well be allowing some sick patients to die unnecessarily."

"Perhaps it is time to look into minimum standards for appointed counsels in death cases." becomes "Perhaps it is time to look into minimum standards for medical care for the indigent."

The article reports that law firms are reluctant to take these cases because "increased profit pressures and large raises for associates deter them . . . They're paying associates $125,000 a year and can't afford to have someone spending 1000 hours on death penalty cases . . ." Finally this shocker: "Firms can save lives and they're not doing enough."

In the field of health care some reforms have already been made—managed care at least has contained medical costs—but so far, unfortunately, this has been done at the expense of good medical care and doctors' incomes.

How about going after the practice of law in this country? As Justice O'Connor says, "Defendants with more money get better legal defense."

What are we waiting for?

## TO THE EDITOR OF NEW YORK MAGAZINE:

## The Un-Hamptons

The article entitled "The Un-Hamptons" in the May issue describes some very interesting and attractive places to visit or have a vacation. What I don't understand, however, is what connection the author was trying to make between the presence of "familiar faces" (by which she meant celebrities) in an area and its attractiveness? Is the idea that their presence makes a place attractive because one can go there to name-drop and hobnob, or is it that one should stay away from such places because as more and more familiar faces arrive more and more scenery-spoiling show-off houses will be built? The article seems ambivalent about these un-spoiled places. How about another article, this time on the "The Un-Un-Hamptons"—attractive places where no familiar faces have arrived yet?

—From a former Shelter Island home-owner, who discovered it for himself when it was still old-fashioned, beautiful and not very chic.

## TO THE EDITOR OF THE NEW YORK TIMES:

## Obscenities in Film

This week the Dow Jones Industrial Average closed at 11,139—a new record high. This, however, does not surpass the number of times four-letter obscenities are used in Spike Lee's porn film *Summer of Sam* or the number of reasons why I am sorry to have spent $8.50 to sit through it and be subjected to what may be the most inarticulate, obscenity-laced and monotonous dialogue in the history of motion pictures. This alleged work of art hits a new low in the exploitation of sex and violence by the entertainment industry.

Our society is simultaneously experiencing incredible economic prosperity and the breakdown of ethical and moral values and what is considered acceptable behavior. Are these two phenomena related in some way? In movies made at the time of the Great Depression of the 1930s no character was allowed to say 'damn' and no crime on screen was allowed to go unpunished.

## TO THE EDITOR OF THE NEW YORK TIMES:

## Bill Clinton Takes Action

At a recent press conference, President Clinton introduced his new anticrime bill, which includes putting 100,000 additional police on the streets of our cities and building a staggering number of new prisons. He then spoke of the tragedy of an 11-year-old schoolgirl who was shot by a 13-year-old schoolboy as she was getting off a school bus. In the same breath he said that the people in the United States enjoyed the greatest freedoms in the world. I doubt that the president was listening to his own speech. In addition to being a free society, this country also jails more of its citizens than any other modern society and we are currently planning to accelerate the process even further! What's so free about being in jail? Other less 'free' societies don't seem to need these drastic measures. What is the explanation for this paradox?

In order for a society to be safe and civilized it is necessary that a majority of its citizens have enough inner controls so that, for the most part, rules are obeyed and laws observed. Naturally, there are those in any society who for a variety of reasons cannot or will not conform or who choose to break rules and laws. These people have to be temporarily removed from society. This serves two purposes: immediate prevention when they are incarcerated and deterrence when they return to society. This approach relies on swift and definite punishment, so that the consequences of crime are fully appreciated.

The United States, however, in its obsession with and zealousness to preserve personal freedoms has invented a number of unique freedoms. Take, for instance, the freedom for adolescents to have babies out of wedlock, something that would have been considered scandalous in earlier times. Nowadays the government actually encourages and protects this freedom by giving support to both mother and child, thereby also protecting the father's freedom to avoid his responsibilities and move on to the next partner.

The father, in fact, is given free condoms at school, which has the effect of encouraging his promiscuity under the guise of protecting him and his partners from AIDS. This policy entirely ignores the fact that the urge to have sex is so strong, especially among the young, that lack of protection is hardly a deterrent. Meanwhile, it only takes once to transmit the HIV virus.

The old excuse that 'you can't stop teenage sex, so at least try to prevent disease' falls flat, in my opinion. The problem requires a different solution. Maybe we should even scare these kids into abstinence until they know what they are doing. Too radical an idea? Well, it would probably save lives. Is a policy to reduce the number of funerals radical?

What about the freedom to buy and sell drugs and become addicted? Anyone can buy just about anything on the streets of New York without fear of police interference. In fact, much of the drug dealing occurs not only with police knowledge, but with police assistance. Read what's in the papers lately and you'll be aghast! Drug treatment seems to be our only answer to this problem, but in fact what's called for are tighter controls on behavior in the period before use and addiction begin. There simply aren't enough drug counselors to even make a dent in the number of Americans who have exercised their freedom to become addicts, and in any case drug treatment is often not very effective. The fact that there exists something we call treatment doesn't mean that it works, and in fact it usually doesn't.

Other questionable freedoms enjoyed by large numbers of honest, law-abiding citizens have become so basic and all-pervasive that we hardly notice them anymore. In New York City for instance, where millions of dollars have been spent to install DON'T WALK signs, you can stand on almost any street corner and observe some very interesting bits of behavior. You will notice first of all that these signs are treated by pedestrians as if they were invisible. This goes for little old ladies with canes and just about everyone else. The sign says DON'T WALK and young mothers push their infants in strollers into the moving traffic. Teenagers weave and dodge between the moving cars like basketball players inventing a new sport. When I wait on the sidewalk for the sign to change I feel like an inhibited, over-obedient jerk, unsophisticated in the ways of the world. If I am behind the wheel of my car entering an intersection with the green light in my favor, I have to be on the lookout for people walking aggressively in front of me, and if I toot my horn I get nothing but dirty looks and four-letter words shouted at me.

And that's at the intersections, where there are lights and crossing signals. In the middle of the block, main thoroughfares in Manhattan are treated like town squares, with people criss-crossing in any direction they please without even looking around, as if there were no such thing as cars. Granted, this phenomenon is largely confined to New York City. In other cities in this country people stare at you if you behave in this way. In some European cities, pedestrians will not cross against a DON'T WALK sign even if there are no cars in sight!

In New York, pedestrians have the freedom to do what they want, when they want, without regard for rules and regulations. If someone questions their behavior, they react angrily, citing the well-worn motto that this is a free country and they can do what they want. A lot of people in this country seem to think that anyone who doesn't do whatever they can get away with is somehow inhibited and not sufficiently self-assertive. Such people themselves, however, seem to be positively obsessed with asserting their freedom as a right, not a privilege.

Turning to the media, we see that things have really gotten out of hand when it comes to the abuse of the concept of freedom. There was a time not so long ago when you couldn't even say the word damn in a movie. Now the so-called F-word has become so pervasive in nearly all media that it is probably the most frequently used word in the language. To some people its indiscriminate use seems to signify freedom of speech! One comedian who was recently taken off the air by two networks claims that he ran all his material by his mother, who not only didn't object to his unbelievably foul language, but thought he was funny! This is a parent?! Another good example is Whoopi Goldberg's rendition of the Star Spangled Banner that was broadcast on cable TV. In it she prefaced every noun in the song with either the F-word or goddamn. It was a disgrace that she did it and it was a disgrace that the network aired it. This formerly very funny and talented performer now uses this kind of language wherever she can get away with it, including on national TV networks. Is this what we mean by freedom of speech—the right to say anything you want, anywhere, at any time? Ridiculous!

There are a host of other typically American freedoms, unfortunately. One is the freedom to do target practice on the streets of our cities, picking off youngsters on the way to school and, if you're really good, hitting them in their beds or doing homework in the living room.

And then there are all those freedoms people can exercise while in their cars. These include driving over the speed limit, driving past someone and shooting them, driving while drunk, driving without a license, going for a ride in someone else's car without asking them, etc. Carjacking is another fast-growing American sport. As for traditional auto theft, fewer than 2% of thieves are convicted, sentenced to jail and incarcerated—an astonishing statistic in this country of car lovers. These crimes are so frequent that the police don't even bother anymore to do anything about them. After all, the insurance companies will pay the owner/victims.

Don't let's forget the freedom to express yourself through urban art masquerading as graffiti, that is, freedom to mess up the scenery for everyone! Then there's the freedom to urinate and defecate in the streets and in lobbies of buildings. After all, what else can you do if there are no public facilities around? It's the city's fault for not building privies all over town.

More freedoms? Freedom to rape! What fun! And to castrate your husband! Freedom to blow your parents away! Whoopee! After all, maybe they weren't nice to you when you were little and spanked you occasionally.

Mugging is another of our freedoms of which so many have taken advantage. In TV sit-coms it's treated as something kind of cute. After all, a guy has to make a living, doesn't he?

THIS IS A FREE COUNTRY, ISN'T IT?

I am not suggesting that the answer is to be found in more or stricter laws. The answer lies in our gaining an understanding of the overwhelming social problems which have gradually beset our country over the course of a long period of neglect. To gain that understanding, it might be useful to ponder a few notions that have been around a while but have been ignored. One has to do with the breakdown of the family and its role in character development. This is where it has to begin. Instead of building prisons, we should insist through public policies that families be encouraged to stay together, supported and held responsible for the basic needs and behavior of their members. Psychologically, human beings need to develop inner controls, and this occurs when parents inculcate values, goals, motivation and respect for—and fear of—authority. The next most important requirement in order for a civilized society to exist is the availability of education and the family's support of it. As former head of the Federal Reserve Alan Greenspan said: "The education of our children will determine the economic future of America."

In other words, we need to address the massive problems that that our society is now facing after years of encouraging freedoms without considering the consequences. Unfortunately, politicians interested in getting votes are generally not interested in major social engineering, since it requires sacrifices that the masses are unwilling to accept.

As for punishment as a deterrent, I can't help but think of all the publicity attending the recent canings in Singapore. What effect is this likely to have on the behavior of foreign visitors to that very safe and orderly city? Will it deter people from engaging in unlawful behavior? If caning would lower the incidence of murder, hijacking and drug dealing in the United States, would it be acceptable as punishment? Would a few strokes of the cane be considered cruel and unusual compared with the suffering of so many innocent victims of crime?

## TO THE EDITOR OF THE NEW YORK TIMES:

## Addiction to Money

In "All This Anger Against the Rich May Be Unhealthy" (October 18, 2009, p. B6) no mention is made of the phenomenon of addiction to money that sometimes afflicts the very rich. It may well be part of what's going on in the case of the hedge fund CEO and his 4 accomplices who were arrested on charges of conspiracy and securities fraud and eventually convicted. The rush, high or elevated feeling of self-esteem that one gets from some drugs can also be triggered by the sudden acquisition of great wealth, whether through success in business, windfall financial gains or winning the lottery. Plus you get to spend the money on expensive cars, enormous yachts and multiple homes to enhance the experience. The overall effect is a strong tendency to equate net worth with self-worth. In the money addict this leads to an uncontrollable need for more wealth that is remarkably similar to a drug addict's need for more drugs. In both cases, trying to get the object of addiction not infrequently leads to bad judgment and self-destructive, even criminal, behavior, as in the case cited above.

I am a psychiatrist and I recall a patient of mine once saying to me "If you have five million, you want 10 million; and if you have 10 million, you need 20 million." The flip side of this is that a significant loss of wealth can result in anxiety, panic and devastating feelings of low self-esteem, depression and, as in the case of one former Enron executive, even suicide. Drug addicts, of course, also engage in self-destructive and criminal behavior and experience equally severe withdrawal effects.

One wonders how much of the current obsession with high-profit financial products and reckless risk-taking in the financial world which is thought to have contributed to the current recession was due to an increase in money-addictive behavior? Some would say it was all due to nothing but greed, but greed is far more common—almost everyone is greedy to some extent—and the merely greedy person is more easily satisfied and less self-destructive than the true addict.

# TO THE EDITOR OF THE NEW YORK TIMES:

## The Recent Incident at Harvard

The recent incident involving the arrest of Harvard University Professor Henry Louis Gates for trying to force entry into his own home ("Charges Against Black Harvard Professor Are Dropped," July 22, 2009, p. A12) was flagrant racial profiling right from the start. A woman called the police to report that "two black men were trying to force entry into a house in the neighborhood." In the first place, how likely is it that burglars are going to break into a house through the front door? And if they had been white, would she have reported that two white men were trying force their way into the house? I doubt it. She obviously thought it unlikely that a house so close to Harvard belonged to a black family, which in effect only compounded the profiling.

## TO THE EDITOR OF THE NEW YORK TIMES: NOVEMBER 7, 2004

## The Pendulum Swings, As Usual

The press is full of post-election articles reporting that President Bush won thanks to the votes of conservative evangelicals from the heartland. As a solid liberal, I was at first disappointed to hear this, but after thinking it over, I realize I am glad the pendulum is swinging in that direction. Over the last few decades we have seen in this country a gradual erosion of people's ability to control their behavior. Society's acceptance of loosened restrictions on sexuality has been accompanied by an increase in aggression and violence as well. This is not surprising, since the two are closely related; open the door to one, and you welcome in the other. Teenage sexual activity has brought with it teenage violence. Just about everyone has been expressing their impulses more and more freely and openly. The same goes for our entertainment, with movies, TV and theater constantly, unremittingly pushing the envelope. One wonders when, if ever, it will stop. Historically, the only way for movement in one direction to be halted is for there to be a reversal and significant, dramatic movement in the opposite direction. I think this will be good for us all; there can be too much freedom and permissiveness in a society. I recall long ago when the movie *Voice of the Turtle* was given an X rating because someone in it said the word 'virgin.' Now they're having intercourse in movies, and the "F-word" has become a normal part of dialogue on the big screen and TV.

## Another Experience of Open-Heart Surgery

After reading Rick Hamlin's account of his unpleasant experience with recovery following open-heart surgery for an aortic valve replacement ("My Heart's Long Surprise," August 8, 2010, Sunday Opinion, p. 9), I am eager to describe my own very different experience, which I hope might allay the fears of those facing the same procedure. I had had an aortic valve replacement at Englewood Hospital in Englewood, New Jersey, on February 24, 2010, when I was already well into my 80s. I had known since I was in my 50s that I had a bicuspid aortic valve, a common congenital defect. It had been under routine monitoring for years and I had had no prior symptoms of cardiac failure.

One day at the office where I practice psychiatry I suddenly felt faint. I got myself to my cardiologist's office in a hurry and two days later underwent open-heart surgery to have my aortic valve replaced and my aortic artery repaired. Sitting up in bed the next day I felt fine, had a good appetite and used the bathroom without help. On the third day I was climbing stairs. On the fifth day I went home and recuperated rapidly enough to return to work after about six weeks, with absolutely no disability. We hired a home health aid for ten days, but she had almost nothing to do. Postoperatively I needed absolutely no pain killers and throughout the whole thing I have taken not even one Tylenol. Two months after the operation I started cardiac rehab, and after two months of that, to the staff's surprise, I was able to work the machines at the highest load level. Through all this I felt just as if nothing had happened to me. I can't believe how easy, non-traumatic and painless it was and liken the experience to that of a minor surgical procedure. The surgery was performed by Dr. James J. Klein, Chief of Cardiac Surgery and his surgical team at the Englewood Hospital, Englewood, New Jersey.

# TO THE EDITOR OF THE NEW YORK TIMES: APRIL 3, 2009

## Obama's Town Hall Meeting

Listening to President Obama's stunningly impressive speech today at the town hall meeting in Strasburg, France, allowed us to experience a political venture unlike any other we have seen in recent memory. The broad sweep of its content included a rundown of the major symptoms of the acute and chronic illnesses of the world community, a diagnosis, a proposed treatment and a prognosis. Two metaphors come to mind. First, Woodrow Wilson's attempts after World War I to establish a League of Nations, and second, Obama as therapist for the family of nations. And from what I gleaned from the goings-on in England over the past two days, the members of the Royal family were all ears and eager to participate. Let's all hope for a successful therapeutic outcome for this dysfunctional world family!

# TO THE EDITOR OF THE NEW YORK TIMES:

## Obama's Notre Dame Speech

In "Debate Obama Hoped to Avoid" (May 15, 2009, p. A14) we are presented with some of the negative reactions to the University of Notre Dame's invitation to President Obama to give the commencement address this Sunday. According to the article, "it has riled opponents of abortion—and the local bishop has vowed to boycott the ceremony."

My suggestion to the President would be to make the topic of his speech "Intolerance of the beliefs of others and its consequences." This would be only fitting, inasmuch as intolerance—especially religious intolerance—is so widespread as to be nearly universal and is the root cause of all the unrest and wars in the world right now, just as it has been over the centuries.

To show how far from simple the moral issue is, in the United States before Roe v. Wade about 15,000 pregnant women died of illegal or self-inflicted abortions *every year*. That means that since 1973 over half-a-million women's lives were saved!

The simplistic, knee-jerk negative reaction to Notre Dame's invitation is just another example of what is really wrong with this world.

## President Obama's Peace Prize

We often hear in the media now that President Obama didn't deserve the Nobel Peace Prize because he, unlike other recipients of the prize, allegedly hasn't done anything tangible in that direction. In my opinion, he has unquestionably contributed to world peace, but his contribution has been of an entirely different and more subtle nature than we have seen before. His is nonetheless a perfectly appropriate and potentially extremely valuable way to address the world's problems: President Obama has offered himself to the world as a sort of family therapist, something the family of nations could certainly use at this point. His gesture has already had the effect of reducing anti-American feelings and inspiring significantly more friendly communication among world leaders, with the result that international tensions are already on the wane. I think that is what the Nobel Committee had in mind.

# TO THE EDITOR OF THE NEW YORK TIMES:

## Reducing the Cost of Medicare

Medicare is a major part of the federal budget. The article "In Health Reform, a Cancer Offers an Acid Test" (July 8, 2009, p. A1) is one of many in the Times recently presenting studies indicating that much of our very expensive medical care produces little or no positive results and is not evidenced-based. It reports, for instance, that the cost of the different treatments for prostate cancer range from $2,436 to $51,069 and the risks of the more invasive (and more expensive) care are not worth the small or "non-existent benefits." In another recent article entitled "26 Billion a Year on Spine Surgery and We Don't Know Whether It Helps" we read that this surgery alone eats up 2.5% of total Medicare costs but "in 85% of back pain cases, we don't know what causes the pain." (In fact, studies have shown that the cause is usually psychosomatic.) Other studies have shown that doctors opt for major surgical interventions such as cardiac bypasses and stents and joint replacements in a significantly varying percentage of cases in different parts of the country and even from hospital to hospital in the same area. In other countries, it is required that conservative medical treatments be tried before major treatments and that surgical interventions be used only as a last resort. If we were to adopt this practice we, too, could probably save large amounts of money without sacrificing the quality of medical care.

## TO THE EDITOR OF NEWSWEEK:

## Treating Back Pain

This week's cover story comes on the heels of an article in the New York Times ("With Costs Rising, Back Pain Often Seems Futile," February 9, 2004) in which it was reported that "a variety of studies have suggested that in 85% of cases it is impossible to say why a person's back hurts." The Newsweek article ends by reporting that a "lone crusader thinks he has the answer" and describes Dr. John Sarno's methods for treating back pain in which he looks into the "inner workings of the mind." It's about time! Those 85 percent of patients referred to earlier are probably suffering from a psychosomatic condition in which, as Sarno points out, their emotional stress and repressed emotions are being expressed in their lower backs.

I am a psychiatrist, and I once had a patient referred to me who was suffering from disabling lower back pain and had been through exhaustive medical examinations, including an MRI and even surgical removal of a superficial fatty tumor on her back, all to no avail. She told me about the pressures in her life: a demanding and critical husband, a demanding full-time job, three young kids and the recent arrival in the household of a demanding and critical mother-in law (this latter being the straw that broke the camel's back, so to speak). At about our eighth session she burst into the office and exclaimed, "I want all those people off my back!" A week later she reported that she had been able to climb a ladder to change the bulbs in a chandelier—without back pain.

Your article points out that although psychotherapy appears to help in some cases, there have been no scientific studies to document its effectiveness as a treatment for back pain. Small wonder! Orthopedists and hospitals would stand to lose all those reimbursements for the $26 billion (!) spent annually in this country on diagnostic and procedures and surgery for back pain.

In my opinion, patients with back pain should spare themselves the usual diagnostic odyssey and start with a visit to a psychiatrist. If it turns out that the most frequent cause of back pain—emotional stress—can be ruled out, the psychiatrist would then refer them to an orthopedist. This would be an easy way to save a large portion of that $26 billion.

## TO THE EDITOR OF THE NEW YORK TIMES:

## The Real Issue in the "Under God" Debate

William Safire's op-ed piece is only the latest in series of contributions in the Times lately to the debate over whether the phrase "under God" should be removed from the Pledge of

Allegiance. In my opinion, this represents a futile last ditch attempt by traditionalists to avert the complete secularization of America. The fact is, though, we're already there.

This has occurred gradually and in many different ways. Our divorce laws are so liberal they have made the process almost do-it-yourself. How many people realize that according to the Bible—much referred to in these matters—if a man divorces his wife, he makes her an *adulteress*, and anyone who marries a divorcee is committing *adultery*? Meanwhile, fornication—which includes *any* sexual behavior outside of marriage by anyone at any age—is such a serious sin that the Bible says (in Corinthians 2) "to avoid fornication, get married, for it's better to marry than to burn." According to scripture therefore, this country is already a land of adulterers and fornicators and is about as awash in sin and secularized as you can get. So really, a little matter of wording in the Pledge of Allegiance is of very little import in the grand scheme of things.

(To my mind, instead of "one nation, under God" what really would be more appropriate would be "one nation, under the Almighty Dollar.")

Bill O'Reilly
Fox News
May 25, 2009

Dear Bill,

I have been a practicing psychiatrist since 1952, when abortion was illegal, and I want to tell you how I see the problem of pro-life vs. pro-choice. In the ongoing debate over the negative consequences of Roe v. Wade—the increase in abortions over the past 35 years—mention is never made of its positive consequences. Prior to 1973, approximately 15,000 pregnant women died every year in the United States due to botched illegal abortions performed either by doctors or by the women themselves using coat hangers. That means that since the decision in Roe v. Wade was handed down in 1973, over half a million women's lives have been saved. Why isn't this statistic mentioned along with the number of legal abortions performed during that period? Meanwhile, it is estimated that 15-20% of all pregnancies end in miscarriage simply through natural spontaneous abortion. Do pro-lifers ever look at this statistic and wonder why this happens and what should or could be done about it? You would think that if they were really interested in saving lives they would be concerned about saving all those fetuses, too. By the way, if fetuses are human beings, why don't churches insist that in cases of miscarriage or abortion the fetuses be baptized and given a Christian burial, rather than discarded in the medical trash bin? Think about it, Bill.

Bill O'Reilly
Fox News
June 7, 2009

Dear Bill,

You're the doctor, Bill, and a woman comes to you in the 3rd trimester of pregnancy and you diagnose eclampsia, which is often fatal to the mother. What do you do? Another woman in the 3rd trimester comes to you who has a fetus with no brain, or some other defect incompatible with life, or Down's syndrome with multiple defects including a heart condition requiring high-risk emergency postnatal open-heart surgery, or other defects, such as missing lower arms and/or legs—there are many such major problems possible. What would you do in these circumstances, save the woman or the fetus? These are the kinds of difficult decisions that obstetricians routinely have to help patients make, and giving sound professional advice is part of providing quality medical care. Under the onslaught of bad publicity, threats, bombings, etc. by 'pro-lifers,' many obstetricians have simply chosen not to take on these sorts of cases any more. That leaves only a few who are willing to provide care to these patients and help them make some of these very difficult medical decisions. Would you be willing, Bill? Before Roe v. Wade, 15,000 women died in the United States every year from botched illegal or self-induced 'coat-hanger' abortions. Do you want to see that happen again?

## TO THE EDITOR OF THE NEW YORK TIMES: SEPTEMBER 12, 2010

### Imam Feisal Rauf Threatens the United States over Building a Mosque near Ground Zero

In an interview with Soledad O'Brien on CNN this evening, Imam Feisal Rauf stated that it would be very dangerous for this country if his proposal to build a mosque and cultural center near Ground Zero in Manhattan was not allowed to go forward. In other words, we better let him do it, or else Muslim extremists will become violent and what happened in Denmark over the anti-Islam cartoon will be child's play in comparison. This is blackmail of the worst kind. It is obvious that he is enjoying and taking advantage of the fact that there are terrorist fringe groups of Muslims on his side when he should be condemning them. He is telling us we'd better not object to this project, or the Muslim world will become incensed and violent and we might be attacked again by Islamic terrorists as on 9/11. This alleged man of peace is threatening us with violence unless we agree to his plan. He said, "Failure to allow this project is dangerous for the United States." In my opinion, Imam Feisal Rauf is the one creating the danger by aligning himself with Islamic terrorists—and he means it!

## TO THE EDITOR OF THE NEW YORK TIMES:

### Our Embarrassing Educational System and What to Do about It Now

Everyone should read Clyde Prestowitz' book *The Great Shift of Wealth and Power to the East*, or if not the book itself then at least the recent review of it in the Times' Book Review Section ("Consider the Outsource," July 3, 2005). It contains, among others, this quote from the book: "China, India, Japan and Europe all churn out more science and engineering degrees than we do. Worse—and downright embarrassing—is the state of American education."

Federal Reserve Chairman Alan Greenspan recently said that the most important thing for our economic future is to catch up with the rest of the world in the education of highly skilled workers. If we are able to muster resources to build the atomic bomb and land on the moon, we ought and need to do the same for the American educational system. It is just as crucial for our future. Unfortunately, in our society professional prestige is directly proportional to income potential, as for example in medicine and law. Prestowitz suggests that one big step toward improving the mess in education would be paying teachers more. How about a project of the same order as the Manhattan Project with massive funding to increase teachers' salaries and upgrade their professional education? That would begin to attract the best students to teaching—which is where they should be in any society anyhow—and eventually teaching would rank along with medicine and law, where it should be. Wouldn't that be wonderful for us all?

# TO THE EDITOR OF THE NEW YORK TIMES:

## The Need for More Good Teachers

Numerous articles in the press have documented and lamented the chronic shortage of teachers in our public schools. Certainly the education of children should be a top priority in our society. However, is it really that there is a shortage of teachers, or is it that there is a shortage of qualified teachers willing to work for the inexcusably low salaries common in the profession, which in addition has little prestige?

Holders of professional degrees in the most prestigious and well paid fields—MDs, LLDs and MBAs—are hardly in short supply. In fact, there are far too many of them. Elevate the teaching profession to the same level of prestige and double current teachers' salaries, and it wouldn't be long before there were plenty of outstanding graduates eager to teach our children in the way they deserve to be taught. What's wrong with a society that hasn't already become aware of this problem and done something about it? Are we really just dumb, are our priorities skewed or is there too much political inertia and lack of resolve to accomplish the task?

While we're talking about the various uses for the anticipated budget surpluses, how about allocating a few billion to raise teachers' salaries to the level of doctors and lawyers? Don't we think our society would be in better shape all around if school teachers were held in high regard and the profession attracted the cream of the crop? Imagine someday there being too many qualified teachers!

A recent article in the Wilson Quarterly entitled "Uneducated Educators" reported on a study that revealed that many school principals are former athletic coaches, etc., and are not really educated to the level they should be. They found that too often the smartest and best educated person in the high school, teachers included, was the valedictorian of the senior class. These are the people who should be going into teaching!

I doubt we will have any trouble getting the very best students attracted to teaching. So many of them now wish they could do something really meaningful and satisfying like teaching, and with the right incentives there would be a crush to get professional teaching credentials. If the list of applicants to educational programs were as long as those for medicine and law, would it improve our educational system? What do you think?

# TO THE EDITOR OF THE NEW YORK TIMES:

## Tom Brokaw Comments

Tom Brokaw ("In search of Truth and Consequences," February 7, 1998) wonders why there is not more outrage over President Clinton's alleged sexual misbehavior. In fact, Clinton's popularity has increased since this whole affair emerged.

Small wonder! It makes good sense to me. Most people, women more than men perhaps, have mixed feelings about extramarital or 'not-in-love' sexual activity. Many are inhibited in this area. Others have these 'lustful desires,' as Jimmy Carter called them, and feel guilty just for having them. Then along comes the President—Big Daddy—who freely satisfies his sexual appetite, apparently without much inner conflict. Not only does he show no signs of guilt or embarrassment, he projects through it all the innocence of a choir boy! What a refreshing relief that must be for anyone who may be suffering doubts and guilt about their own desires or behavior.

Remember when Jimmy Swaggart was caught in illicit extramarital sexual behavior and loudly proclaimed his guilt, confessed his sins and agonized about it on TV, begging forgiveness from his God and everyone else? He was of no help to anyone!

The increased popularity of the President appears to me to be related to the fact that he exudes humanity and by his guilt-free attitude exonerates all those who may be in conflict about their sexual desires and behavior, according to the principle "If the President is like that, I guess I'm not so bad after all."

## TO THE EDITOR OF THE NEW YORK TIMES:

### President Bush and Invading Iraq

Why did he do this to us?
Was it to be a 'wartime president?'
Or because Saddam Hussein tried to kill his daddy?
Or for Jesus? (Jesus has enough wars to his credit.)
Or to show up his daddy?
Or just because he wanted to?
Or maybe even he himself doesn't know why he did it.
He just did it.
And as he said about the insurgents, "Bring 'em on!"
That's a good one!
Sounds like he likes a good fight.
Who will be the McNamara of this war?
Condoleezza Rice?
Anybody have the answers?

## TO THE EDITOR OF THE NEW YORK TIMES:

### Hummer SUVs

The article in today's Times about Hummer SUVs (April 5, 2003, p. C1) exemplifies the remarkable diversity of opinion one finds in this country. The article contains, among others, this incredible statement by the founder of a Hummer owners group: "The H2 is an American icon . . . It's a symbol of what we all hold so dearly above all else . . . Those who deface the Hummer in word or deed deface the American flag." The American flag, no less! The author of the article reports that some Hummer owners "feel patriotic behind the wheel"—just as if they were with our forces invading Iraq! In my opinion, the Hummer is threatening and militaristic in appearance and absurdly oversized. If they ever really became popular, our highways would look like battlefields. It would also confirm in the minds of those abroad who already see America as a militaristic bully and policeman to the world that their perceptions are correct. I think these gas-guzzling, road-hogging vehicles are an obscenity and an embarrassment to our country and should be prohibited anywhere trucks are not allowed, such as on parkways. Arnold Schwarzenegger, ex-governor of California, is said to have five of these vehicles in different colors for his personal use.

## TO THE EDITOR OF THE NEW YORK TIMES: MAY 4, 2005

During a recent visit to France it became apparent to me that the automobile is viewed there as a means of transportation rather than a trophy of financial success or an ego trip. I have seen ads in the United States for an SUV that describe it as fearless. In France, the rare humongous American SUV that one encounters is more like an obscenity alongside the compact, practical cars that dominate the scene. Far from being fearless, these huge American cars can barely maneuver through the narrow streets in French cities and towns.

I visited a local Lincoln dealership recently where a Lincoln Navigator, billed as "the most powerful and luxurious SUV on the planet," was on display. I told the salesman that in my opinion it shouldn't be allowed on the road. To my surprise, he agreed with me! Mr. Ford of the eponymous corporation opined recently that these huge vehicles are both dangerous and bad for the environment. When someone then asked him why his company continued to make and sell them, his answer was that he was beholden to his stockholders!

These large SUVs are really small trucks and should be treated as such and excluded from our restricted parkways so that drivers of normal cars don't have to put up with the tailgating and aggressive driving of SUV owners and the blinding lights of their monster vehicles. SUVs have been shown to cause more deaths than smaller cars in accidents.

The French also have zero tolerance for cell phone use while driving and treat it as an offense no less serious than DWI. Conviction can result in a prison term of up to 6 months.

The problem is that too many people in our 'free society' here in America won't tolerate restrictions on behavior they are used to and enjoy so much, and legislators will not dare risk trying to pass restrictive legislation for fear of displeasing voters. Perhaps a grassroots movement might be able to bring some sanity and good judgment to these subjects.

## TO THE EDITOR OF THE NEW YORK TIMES:

## Keep SUVs Away from Automobiles

The author of a recent article in the Times (February 8, 2011, p. A15) interviewed the owner of a "gas-guzzling, smog-inducing, planet-warming, road-hogging" SUV who calls her vehicle her "armor" and says "the world is becoming a harder and more violent place to live, so we wrap ourselves with these big vehicles. It's like riding a horse. You have more power." Another says "It gives you a barrier, makes you feel less threatened." In actuality, these two SUV lovers themselves are making a significant contribution to the violence they perceive, given that in another article (January 30, p. C1) the Times reports statistical evidence that "large pickups and large SUVs cause significantly higher death rates in other-vehicle accidents with cars than do smaller vehicles."

I have two suggestions to make. The first is that SUV owners who share the attitudes expressed by these two women should seek psychiatric help for their anxiety and paranoid tendencies and second, that those who drive ordinary automobiles be afforded some protection from SUVs by eliminating these dangerous vehicles from all parkways now designated for passenger vehicles only. After all, large pickups and SUVs are really trucks and should be registered and regulated as trucks.

## TO THE EDITOR OF THE NEW YORK TIMES:

### The Chevrolet Avalanche

The Chevrolet Avalanche is the latest addition to the list of gas-guzzling, air—polluting SUVs on the market. In black, it looks like something Darth Vader would drive. Its appearance is by design menacing and dangerous—even the name suggests deadly violence. I would like to suggest an new acronym for these absurdly oversized Menacing and Dangerous Vehicles: MADVs.

Bill Maher recently remarked to Larry King on TV that displaying an American flag on one's SUV would be the very least one could do for the war effort. But just wait until you see GM's new domesticated Hummer! Originally an aggressive-looking, out-sized military vehicle, it's now being offered in an even bigger version luxuriously outfitted for family use by upscale suburban soccer moms! I suppose, though, for real cachet in wartime nothing stills beats a surplus Sherman Tank!

## TO THE EDITOR OF THE NEW YORK TIMES:

The Times recently reported a fatal accident in Pennsylvania in which a teenage driver lost control of an SUV on a curve and the vehicle rolled over several times, killing three of the occupants. This is just another in the increasing number of such accidents involving unstable SUVs. The government requires that all toys that might cause injury or death to children carry a warning label. Isn't it about time that SUVs with a high center of gravity and propensity to roll over also have warning labels? It could read "Warning! Driving this vehicle over 40 miles per hour is dangerous and may result in a fatal accident." Then let's see what happens to the SUV craze and what Detroit does about it.

## TO THE EDITOR OF THE NEW YORK TIMES: MARCH 5, 2011

### Stuttering and *The King's Speech*

After seeing the movie *The Kings Speech* and reading in the Times about research on stuttering and treatments for it, I would like to share my own experience and opinion on the subject. Although I was a moderately severe stutterer through childhood and into early adulthood, it did not deter me from pursuing a career in psychiatry which I have been able to practice successfully for nearly fifty years. A psychoanalyst named Smiley Blanton wrote a book in the 1940s called *For Stutterers* in which he explained the psychodynamics of the disorder. He also treated many stutterers, including myself, with considerable success. But it wasn't until I underwent on-the couch psychoanalysis that I really understood the dynamics underlying the affliction, and following that the stuttering virtually disappeared. (Interestingly, it actually persisted for quite a while, but only during analytic sessions, as the dynamics were becoming clearer.)

All these many years I have had no problem at all in my practice or elsewhere. I do sometimes experience very briefly remnants of the symptom under certain circumstances, usually when I am aware of some sort of minor conflicting emotions in myself. But even then my stuttering is barely noticeable to anyone but me. It's an interesting fact that stutterers don't stutter when they are expressing anger, speaking in a foreign language or speaking out loud alone in a room. My most vivid memory in this connection is of the time I was practicing to give the valedictory speech at my high school graduation. I could hardly talk and the teacher asked me what we should do. I told her not to worry, I would be all right; and sure enough, the speech went off without a hitch, much to everyone's surprise.

In my opinion, the causes of stuttering are essentially psychological, not physical or neurological. The fact that the King and his therapist remained good friends for the rest of their lives, both in the movie and in real life, indicates to me that the therapeutic effect was largely psychological and that the relationship between the two was crucial to the outcome.

## The Case of Congressman Wiener

The dramatic so-called scandal of Congressman Wiener's public revelations of his own inappropriate behavior would be readily understandable if he were 16 years old, because that's how old he is behaving. Most people who appear outwardly successful in their profession are just what they appear to be, i.e., adults who reached maturity on schedule. But there are also many people who, despite outwardly appearing to be successful adults, were actually stuck in their psychological development before they reached adulthood. That is, significant aspects of a person's psychological makeup get stuck somewhere between early childhood and one's teens, and then remain at that level of development while the person outwardly grows into an adult. This is what we recognize in the old joke "the only difference between boys and men is the price of their toys." It is a very widespread phenomenon, which I also encounter frequently in my psychiatric practice, and to describe it I have coined the term Predominant Maturational Age Identity.

By 'identity' I mean the way one perceives and feels about oneself. Every person has some degree of multiple identity, but it's a matter of how much of one's psychology and behavior it influences. I have treated grown women who tell me "I feel like a little girl." One man, a highly successful 29-year-old businessman, told me "I've felt like a teenager ever since I was one." These people's experience of themselves has nothing to do with their adult lives or their real age.

In other words, there is a disconnect between who they are and how they experience themselves. And when behavior from their immature identity comes out, it seems inappropriate, if not bizarre, and is often incomprehensible, as in the case of Representative Wiener.

# Chapter 9

## ESSAYS

THE FOLLOWING ESSAYS ARE ON a variety of subjects which have aroused my interest and prompted me to put my ideas in print. Most have to do with the striking changes that have taken place in American culture in the last few decades. Many things that are experienced by the majority of Americans alive today, especially the younger generation, as perfectly normal and acceptable are experienced by members of the older generation as striking and sometimes shocking changes compared with the culture we grew up with. Different generations typically have conflicting views of the world and its characteristics, and I do not wish here to be judgmental or otherwise intolerant of all that is new. But sometimes even rapid changes in social attitudes and habits take place unheeded by most people until someone points out how striking they really are. Then even the most modern and tolerant person may recognize the need for our society to reflect on, and possibly change or even reject some of what has taken place.

# The Automobile, the All-American Fetish

The modern automobile, aside from supplying transportation, satisfies a long list of fantasies, wishes, psychological needs and outlets that have nothing to do with transportation. The fulfillment of these secondary needs, however, actually takes precedence over the most important attribute of an automobile, namely, safety. I invite you to consider the following.

1. Aesthetics. There is no doubt that physical appearance is one of the chief factors that makes an automobile desirable and therefore marketable. Ugly cars don't sell; beautiful ones do. There exists an entire vocabulary for the description of automotive designs: sweeping, rakish, etc. During the Depression of the 1930s what we now call classic cars were practically works of art, exquisitely designed and extremely expensive, and are now just as highly valued as other fine art antiques.

2. Status. As a socio-economic status symbol, the automobile ranks second only to one's home in announcing to the world that one has arrived. A Rolls Royce cannot be trumped except perhaps by the new Mercedes Benz Maybach at a quarter of a million. The less ostentatious among the very rich chose the modest Bentley over the showy Rolls.

There was a time when General Motors automobiles were more differentiated in size; now they don't vary much in size, only in level of luxury and cost. In those days GM models went all the way from the small, inexpensive Chevrolet through the mid-sized brands Pontiac, Olds and Buick, all the way up to the big, luxuriously appointed Cadillac, which usually cost many times more than a Chevrolet, especially the custom-made jobs. A relative of mine who worked for GM in the old days told me that a GM manager could not be seen driving a model higher on this scale than his boss. When I had my first job in a hospital I drove a 'pre-owned' Cadillac (in those days the term was 'second-hand'), which ruffled the feathers of the director of the hospital, who drove a mere Buick.

He would make snide remarks about "that young doctor who drives a Cadillac!"

3.  Virility. As a symbol of virility, the automobile is hardly less evocative than one's actual sexual apparatus, which cannot be openly displayed in our culture. Young men prefer sports cars, anything from a Corvette to a Ferrari, whereas the average age of a Cadillac buyer is 67. In the old days, the Pontiac was a car for old-maid school teachers. Young women go for a man with a snazzy sports car—it says a lot about a man, or so the women believe. They're definitely not interested in one who drives a Chevrolet sedan. One sometimes also sees older men trying to recapture their youth by driving a convertible sports car, a Corvette for example. (It's not as effective as Viagra, however!)

4.  Power. Close in importance to virility is power. The popularity of the SUV seems largely due to the commanding driving position which creates the gratifying illusion of power and dominance over normal passenger cars. The fact that SUVs are more heavily constructed and cause more deaths in collisions with passenger cars doesn't seem to be considered a disadvantage. (A local Lincoln salesman agreed with me that the Lincoln Navigator shouldn't actually be allowed on the road.) Women in particular seem to enjoy the feeling of power they get from driving these road monsters. However, as the number of SUVs on the road increases, the feeling of physical superiority will diminish. The recent publicity about the Ford Explorer's tendency to roll over owing to its high center of gravity says a lot more than I could about the design priorities at work in these vehicles.

5.  Speed. This is another attribute that figures strongly in the thinking of automakers and buyers alike. Auto magazines in their evaluations of new cars always include the number of seconds a car takes to accelerate from 0 to 60 miles per hour. While it is true that this gives an indication of performance, I'd like to know where on our streets and highways is it advisable or even legal to accelerate from 0 to 60 mph in 6 or 8 seconds?

An elderly relative of mine once boasted that his Cadillac with a Northstar engine could go 145 mph. I refrained from saying that I doubted he would ever think of going that fast and that I hoped he wouldn't demonstrate the car's capabilities with me in it. As for the appeal of speed among young people, one well-known, rational and very admired professional tennis player, speaking of his recent purchase of a high-performance sports car, said "what 25-year-old doesn't like speed?" (Please, not on the local roads!) Young men in any kind of car like to experience the rush of fast driving, too often with lethal consequences, as we all know. The fastest anyone needs to drive or should drive is 75 mph, and then only on open roads under the most favorable conditions. So what is the point of making cars that do 145 mph or 125 mph—or even 85 mph?

6. Performance. In the minds of car enthusiasts this is perhaps a car's most important attribute. Acceleration, top speeds, cornering, road feel and steering accuracy are all considered important, particularly so in sports cars. The very term sports car suggests athleticism: the virtues of agility, speed, power, maneuverability, braking, etc. And yet, unlike athletic fields or basketball courts, public roads are no place for exhibiting high performance. Somewhere on Long Island there is actually an obstacle course where SUV owners can take their prized power-car possessions and put them through their paces. It's apparently popular with trophy-conscious SUV owners who want to see if they got their money's worth. Once at the course a Range Rover owner misjudged the size of one of the mounds and rolled his vehicle over. He was not happy.

7. Style. As a fashion statement, a car is second only to clothes in its ability to signal the latest trend. Automobile styles used to undergo major changes on a yearly basis. Now only minor changes are made yearly, with major changes being made every five years. It is still the case these days, however, that to successfully market a car automakers have to tout each year's new features, both in order to make previous years' models

appear obsolete more quickly and, equally important, to give buyers a way to let everyone know they just bought a new car.

8. Image. Of all the attributes of automobiles, one of the most important to the buying public seems to be the overall image a car projects. No matter how attractive a car is, how many people would you expect to buy it if it's called a Buick Rose or a Cadillac Rodent? The list of names that would destroy a car's marketability and doom it to oblivion is very long. There is no doubt that names like Mustang, Cherokee and Range Rover add to an automobile's appeal; these are names, along with many others, that can easily be dropped in conversation. On the other hand, hearing that someone drives a Viper makes one's ears prick up. (These owners don't bother to name the car company that makes it—it's not a prestigious one—and if you don't already know it, your opinion doesn't count anyway.) Interestingly, the really expensive luxury cars don't seem to need compelling names to attract buyers. They are usually designated with letters or numbers. The Mercedes E320 says all it needs to say without calling it a Mercedes Spitfire, or something similar. That is, the nameplate alone has enough cachet for the affluent buyer. Lexus, BMW and Infiniti handle it the same way, whereas Lincoln seems to need actual names to bolster the image of its cars. (Then again, it's really not in the same class as the other three.)

In Europe, Mercedes designates their models using numbers below 100, but so as not to appear outdone by the Japanese Lexus, which uses numbers in the hundreds, Mercedes models destined for the American market are also assigned numbers in the hundreds. After all, who would want to park a Mercedes 30 alongside a Lexus 300 at the country club? Perhaps not surprisingly, car jockeys at country clubs are actually under instructions to park the cars according to make, the more expensive ones nearer the clubhouse and the lesser ones, like Ford and Chevrolet, far away. A Rolls or Bentley is automatically parked right at the front door.

9. Freedom. Many people feel much freer to express themselves when they get behind the wheel of a two-ton enclosed object like a car, where they are for the most part protected from retaliation. In their cars, quiet and inhibited people can become cursing monsters, capable of spewing strings of four-letter words they would never be caught using otherwise. Road rage, an especially uncivilized and dangerous contemporary phenomenon, has become almost commonplace. A recent study in New Jersey indicated that about 40% of drivers are in a state of anger while driving. Anger is known to impair reason and judgment, so an angry person controlling a powerful and lethal weapon is very dangerous.

10. Safety. Until recently, automakers haven't taken much interest in safety because they know it is not as important to the auto-buying public as the other factors listed above. A former CEO of GM admitted on TV recently that his company was now concentrating on quality, since that is where some of the foreign companies seemed to be concentrating. American automakers used to rely on built-in obsolescence rather than durability to maintain high sales volumes. And of course, in a capitalist society public demand makes for profits, and corporations can and do simply point out that they are giving the public what it wants.

One of the first major safety improvements was safety glass, which arrived in most cars in the 1930s. Before that, only windshields might been made of safety glass. Accidents back then were correspondingly more bloody than they are today, though not as lethal overall because speeds were slower. Seat belts, which became standard some years ago, represented a major change in the attitudes of automakers. Then came airbags, reinforced cabin structure and other safety improvements. These developments notwithstanding, automobile design has for the most part not been dominated by the aim to make cars as safe as possible.

In Europe, where gasoline prices are two or three times higher than in America, the luxury to indulge in most of the psychologically motivated design features we take for granted doesn't exist. In Europe, many of the cars are designed with gas consumption in mind, whereas in America this is barely a consideration except as necessary to comply with government requirements. (Imagine what would happen if gasoline was taxed here the way it is in Europe and cost $7.00 a gallon. It would start a second American revolution!) A small European car, with its low weight and flimsy construction, would be dangerous to drive on American highways because it would be clobbered in an accident with even an average-size American car. Conversely, most American cars can't be driven in at least some parts of Europe because of the narrow roads, both in the cities and in the country. Over there, automakers have to produce cars that are practical rather than ornamental or athletic. There's hardly any market in Europe for the gas-guzzlers we in America like to indulge ourselves in. I was once riding in a Mercedes taxi in Paris (most taxis in France and Germany are Mercedes) and I mentioned to the driver that in America only the rich drive Mercedes. His surprised response was "What about a Chevrolet?"

Our preoccupation with designing automobiles based on the various psychological and aesthetic factors described above—our automobile fetish—comes at a very high price. This includes tens of thousands of deaths in highway accidents every year, an even greater number of maimed and disabled, and of course enormous costs associated with property damage, insurance premiums, litigation, etc.

What if someone designed a car primarily for safety without regard to appearance, cachet, esthetics, speed, performance, maneuverability, power, status, sexiness or any of the other qualities people seem to want most? Would it be possible to reduce the carnage and high cost of automobile travel as we know it? Could the interior be made from some sort of very strong plastic and be lined with a cushioning that would prevent serious injury in a crash? Could one install a device to limit speed and acceleration and an alarm that would go off if the car in front got too close? (Tailgating causes more accidents than any other behavior on the road. The safe following distance of one car length for every 10 mph is universally ignored.)

The main argument against these proposals is that cars designed this way would be too expensive and people wouldn't buy them.

Such cars would be nothing more than a means of transportation, and people wouldn't be motivated to buy them since they would lack everything car buyers value and look for: cachet, status, image, fashion, status, power, speed, sex appeal, etc. For people to be willing to design and buy cars simply for transportation and keep them as long as they worked for that purpose and were reasonably comfortable, there would have to be a major shift in attitudes. And, just as important, people would have to find some other arena in which to satisfy all the wishes, fantasies and needs currently satisfied by cars. This could be clothes, jewelry, boats, airplanes, hobbies, art—anything where fashions change so that there is always something new that everyone wants/needs to have in order to keep up with the crowd, prove his or her worth or show off.

What if the production and widespread use of safe automobiles could save tens of thousands of lives each year, prevent many more thousands of accidents resulting in serious injury and disfigurement and save millions, if not billions, of dollars—would it be worth it? Of course! Will it or could it ever be done? Of course not! It would so disrupt existing manufacturing systems and cause such legal and legislative controversy that it would never get to first base. One can easily imagine what would happen to lawmakers who tried to pass a law requiring automakers to produce cars in which the overriding consideration was safety and all the other qualities required by America's love affair with the automobile were ignored. They would be voted out faster than you could accelerate a hot BMW from 0 to 60.

That's our democracy! It doesn't always deliver what is best for everyone, a good example being the modern automobile.

FLASH! July 30, 2011. President Obama has just reached an agreement with American automobile manufacturers to increase the average fuel efficiency of cars to 54.5 mpg, about twice the present figure, by the year 2025. This will obviously require smaller, lighter and less powerful cars. A lighter material, perhaps a durable plastic, will probably need to be developed for use in the body. There is no doubt that the traditional American automobile will have to be drastically redesigned and reengineered and will barely resemble what we now see on the roads. A variety of alternate fuels are being developed to decrease our dependence on petroleum, including vegetable oil products. We now have hybrid electrics, electric plug-ins, vehicle powered by vegetable oil and a few hydrogen fuel cell models—all of which are at present prohibitively expensive. The American automobile is about to experience a major metamorphosis into something more efficient, less suitable as an object of affection, and no longer capable of meeting the psychological needs that present models fulfill. The large luxury sedans and SUVs will gradually fade into the sunset. American automobiles of the future will come to resemble their European cousins, with the emphasis on fuel economy and safety.

## The Practice of Psychiatry

I have been practicing psychiatry since the late 1940s, a time when there were virtually no psychotropic medications available for the treatment of mental disorders and about all we had was electroshock. Over the decades I have witnessed our armamentarium grow to include a remarkable array of pharmacological agents. The so-called antipsychotic medications arrived in this country in the mid-fifties, as did the first generation of antidepressants. These were joined over the following years by the MAOs (monoamine oxidases) and a few others. Although quite effective, these medications had the disadvantage that they were slow-acting and had significant undesirable side effects that often precluded their use or led to a lot of non-compliance. Since the introduction of the modern generation of antidepressants, however, beginning 25 years ago with Prozac, the treatment of most emotional illnesses, that is, diseases of the brain, has taken giant steps forward. I call these new medications 'brain normalizers.'

The new medications seem to be effective in correcting not only symptoms, but also chronic characterological problems, something which practitioners of traditional psychoanalysis believed could be accomplished only with their particular treatment modality. Some psychoanalysts are so narrow in their views that they go so far as to completely dismiss the value of dynamic psychotherapy, the most common variety of interpretative psychotherapeutic treatment. Whereas psychoanalysis is traditionally conducted without eye contact between analyst and patient (who may be on a couch) and is focused on the patient's fantasies and interpretation of the transference, dynamic psychotherapy is usually conducted vis-à-vis and is characterized by a stronger emphasis on the patient's present situation and its origins in the past and by greater involvement on the part of the therapist, who offers the patient more positive ego support.

The two questions I am most frequently asked by friends, relatives and strangers alike are "How can you stand dealing with all those nuts?" (or some other pejorative term for psychiatric patients) and "What is the most common problem people come to you with for treatment?"

The first question is easy; the second is harder. There is still a lot of prejudice and stigma associated with emotional illness. Such terms a 'those neurotics' or 'those psychotics' are used pejoratively and tend to stigmatize people with psychiatric disorders. One never hears 'those diabetics' or 'those arthritics' used in a pejorative sense. People with diabetes or arthritis are thought of as normal people who happen to have a medical condition, whereas people with mental disorders are thought of as having a fundamentally weak or flawed character rather than as being afflicted with a disorder of the brain. A common attitude is that they should pull themselves up by their own bootstraps without needing psychiatric treatment.

People who espouse these attitudes often say they don't believe in psychiatry. This makes about as much sense as saying that one doesn't believe in dentistry. Such people either believe that psychiatry is not a legitimate medical specialty or else they don't believe psychiatry helps anyone. Either way it shows gross ignorance and prejudice.

I respond by saying that most of my patients are highly intelligent and often quite successful in their work (by which I am referring to competence more than earnings); they are aware of being stuck in some area or areas of their lives in a way that prevents them from experiencing full satisfaction and a feeling of accomplishment; and they are motivated to varying degrees to do something about it, or else they wouldn't come to me for help. Typically they have done some introspection and have already gained some initial insight on their own, unless urgent psychic pain (usually depression or anxiety) has driven them to seek relief. In sum, they are, like medical patients generally, people who are experiencing some sort of problem or distress that they haven't been able to overcome on their own.

I have noticed after many years of treating patients that there is one other striking feature common to most. There are two ways I can describe this. One is that these are people who don't really know who they are or, if they do know intellectually, they don't experience themselves as they really are. The other way of putting it is that psychologically these people are stuck in their own past; that is, their ideas, perceptions, behavior patterns and attitudes about themselves and others have not changed as they have grown older. As Robert Burns put it in his poem *To a Louse*: "O wad some Power the giftie gie us / To see oursels as ithers see us!" My patients are people who really have no idea how others see them.

I describe the phenomenon as living life on two tracks. On the one hand, there is the operational or reality track on which the person has relationships, marries, raises kids, is successful, achieves career goals, etc. and is perceived by others as having accomplished all these things. The other track is the subjective experience track, which in these patients bears little relation to the reality track.

Here are a few examples. One six-foot-four-inch, impressive, successful businessman with a good marriage and a healthy son described a meeting with other men in which he felt "out of place—like a little boy." His own dysfunctional family had impeded his psychological growth, but outwardly he was able to live what others would consider a normal adult life. His father actually told him at an early age that he was sorry that he had ever had a son and that he, the son, would never amount to anything. Meanwhile this man, my patient, was a popular Little League baseball coach who was adored by his teams and respected by the players' parents. He, meanwhile, lived in fear that the adults around him suspected him of being a pedophile, and this despite the fact that he never experienced or displayed the slightest indication of such tendencies.

Another patient was a highly successful foreign-born businessman who had come to this country with his parents, worked in their business and then gone into business for himself and amassed a fortune in real estate. He earned in the high six figures, and when I said to him, "You really are a successful business man," he replied, "I don't see it that way. I don't feel financially secure. Only if my wife's family had millions would I feel financially secure." His father had told him as a child that he would never be successful, and he had always felt intimidated by his older brothers, despite the fact that in adulthood he had surpassed them all professionally and in other ways. He genuinely couldn't experience any of this and was convinced that even much less accomplished men would look down on him.

I once treated a well-educated, professionally successful married woman who when she was young had had many friends, had experienced constant praise from teachers and had been admired and envied by other girls in school, but who apparently had caused problems for her parents at home through her constant demands for attention and love. She had been sent to psychiatrists since an early age and had been in and out of treatment unsuccessfully over the years. Her problem when she came to me, at about age thirty, was that she felt unable to make decisions about anything without first asking her domineering mother. She did not experience herself as having accomplished the things she had in fact accomplished. She felt she was a basket case, plagued by fears, panic states and intense anxiety. She reported that growing up at home she had been called a devil, a bad seed and an impossible child, even though at school her teachers had always described her as a model student. She felt like a failure, and doubted that she could get on in the world without her mother. With treatment, she began to show improvement.

I had another woman come to me once with an extreme case of what we call body dystrophic disorder. She was stunningly attractive and could have been on the cover of any fashion magazine, but she was convinced she was ugly and was saving up for a nose job, a chin job, eye jobs, breast augmentation and liposuction of the stomach. She described her legs as "the ugliest in the world." Although her boyfriend told her otherwise, she "knew he was lying." All she wanted from me was Prozac, since in her mind that was the only way she could bear to live with such an ugly body, and when I suggested she have some therapy to try to understand why she had these feelings, she protested that they were the truth, not feelings that could be changed through therapy.

Another patient, a middle-aged housewife who had successfully raised three children, always felt she had to please everyone but herself because she was inadequate and a failure. She put up with intimidating and demeaning treatment from everyone in the family, had very low self-esteem and was in general hesitant to socialize with others. She never felt she was a normal adult woman who deserved respect and could hold her own with family members and friends. Instead, she identified as an emotionally retarded child masquerading as an adult. She was simply incapable of seeing herself as a beloved grandmother and successful mother, though that is what she was.

And then there was the psychiatrist who came to me as a patient, a highly intelligent, educated and well trained professional who taught courses and lectured in addition to his clinical work. Once during treatment he complained "You're trying to make a psychiatrist out of me!" This upset him because, as he explained, he hated his work, felt it had been a mistake to go into the field and wished he could do something else. When I pointed out to him that he *was* a psychiatrist he replied, "But I don't feel like one. I don't identify as a psychiatrist. My family wouldn't let me do what I wanted and I just went into psychiatry to please them." This man was competent, hardworking and respected as a clinician, but he had done everything possible to deny his accomplishments and sabotage his own progress, which had resulted in his having repeatedly lost his job.

Another patient was a handsome, socially popular and professionally successful single man in his late thirties who realized that he was all these things and had a lot to offer a prospective mate. His problem was that he realized these things only intellectually. In his heart he felt and believed that no woman could possibly choose him over another man, and that even if one did profess love for him, she would in reality continue to think about other men she might meet. In his own family he had never known any love and recalled receiving only negative comments from his mother and father. He could attract women with ease and had had sex with at least a hundred, and yet he didn't feel he was sexually desirable and as a consequence had never allowed himself to become emotionally involved or committed.

Then there was this patient: male, brilliant Harvard graduate, M.D. from a prestigious medical school, partner in a highly respected practice, married to an accomplished woman, father of two sons, in the process of having a new house built. He told me he felt as if he hadn't done anything with his life. He asked me whether the life he had was all he could look forward to, and that if so, he felt like a failure. When I listed everything he had going for him and all that he had accomplished, he replied, "But I don't feel it. I don't feel like I'm a doctor." He compared himself to his friends who had made millions in business and felt that since he had not, he had done nothing worthwhile with his life.

Another case: a highly respected and highly paid computer programmer who was in a stable live-in relationship with a successful young woman. Although he acknowledged his own abilities, be couldn't genuinely believe that his girlfriend loved him or that his friends wanted him around. It turned out he had been an angry and rebellious adolescent. His father, himself an angry and hostile character, never had had any respect for him and still didn't. His mother had even once said to him she was sorry she had ever had children. The patient told me he thought of himself as being full of hostility, which in his mind made him undesirable as a friend or a lover.

The common thread in all of these patients is the wide discrepancy between who they really are and how they experience themselves—their identity. The therapeutic goal for all such patients is to reduce this disconnect between who they are and how they identify themselves so that they can begin to experience their real selves. It's quite difficult, however, to change a person's self-perception if it was already strongly negative in childhood owing to the family situation. As the saying goes, "We are living out our childhood traumas."

# Business Newscasters' Big Mouths

The popular business newscasters, especially those on CNBC Business, seem to enjoy mobilizing as much fear and anxiety as possible in their investor viewers by using terms and metaphors aimed at dramatizing everything and scaring everybody. Pessimism is their stock-in-trade (excuse the pun). Downward moves in the market or individual stocks are frequently reported using such terms as *plunged, sell-off, slaughtered, plummeted, hammered, taken out and shot, carnage, blood-letting, caught in the downdraft, tech-wreck* and *tanked*—to name a few. If the Dow dropped a few points it *tumbled.* For an up-day, however, we typically only hear that the price *rose,* had an *up-day* or perhaps *soared,* thought this latter is often spoken in a tone tinged with something like disappointment. When reporting a 7-point drop in the Dow, they say the Dow fell *almost 7 points,* rather than the Dow fell *only 7 points.* Playwrights know that dark and tragic stories are more interesting to audiences than wholesome and upbeat ones. Bad news, just like tragedy, provides more drama, and business news editors make the most of it. As one newscaster put it, "We in the media prefer to report bad news—it's more dramatic."

Well, I have some suggestions for business news broadcasters that might help them make people's lives even more scary and miserable. When the news is bad, why not talk about a *holocaust?* Why not use even more juicy metaphors to describe stocks that lost value: *murdered, bludgeoned, machine-gunned, eviscerated, dismembered, decapitated, disemboweled, executed, castrated, amputated, under the knife, vomited up, struck by lightning, about to get last rites, dumped in the sewer, raped, fell into quicksand, H-bombed, eaten by sharks, thrown to the piranha fish, run over by a steamroller?* (I could go on, but you get the idea.) I'm sure if they really put their minds to it they could come up with even more offensive and frightening terms—then just watch the ratings soar!

As I was writing this I heard on CNBC that Eaton Corp. stock was *"eaten away"*—they're getting the idea! How about General Electric was *electrocuted*! or Compaq was dumped in the *trash compactor*! or

IBM was *machine-gunned*! or Merrill Lynch was *lynched*! And I can't wait to hear someone someday say Krispy Kreme was *cremated*! But why stop there? They should have a nationwide contest to see who can come up with the most shocking and frightening terms for use by our media sweethearts.

We know that news commentators traditionally prefer to report stories of disasters and other bad news, but the business commentators I have in mind take biased reporting to a whole new level. They take visible delight in using misleading metaphors, hyperbole and an ominous tone of voice to exaggerate negative news out of all proportion, knowing that raising the anxiety level has the effect of attracting viewership.

Ironically, in a period when the stock markets overall have climbed to unprecedented levels in record time, beyond everyone's wildest dreams, any minor drop in the market is reported as a *plunge*. But plunged actually means something different, as in the diver *plunged* into the ocean and disappeared from view. Compare 'the market *sank* 2% today' with 'the Titanic *sank* to the bottom of the ocean.' Similarly, one often hears that there was a *sell-off* of 2½ percent, whereas a sell-off actually means something more like a *liquidation sale*. Yesterday, we heard there had been a *biotech bust*, which it turns out was merely a correction in the prices of stocks which had risen dramatically over the previous few weeks. In this case, the decline was in response to remarks by President Clinton about placing genome information in the public domain. That morning, one analyst had already upgraded the biotech company Amgen, one of the *busted* biotech stocks, to 'strong buy.' Another news outlet flashed the headline "Biotechs Wasted."

Other scare tactics include graphics of large red arrows pointing downward, indicating a *plunge* or *sell-off* of maybe 2 or 3 percent—typically following a run-up orders of magnitude larger! You sometimes even hear *nose-dive* used to describe a drop of 2%! It goes without saying that instead of saying the market fell *less than* 2% today, they say (with ominous inflection) the market fell *nearly* 2% today. When the market rises, one sometimes even gets the impression that the commentators report it grudgingly, as if they were disappointed not to be able to say something negative.

After a bad day in the markets they call in 'experts' to discuss such loaded and wildly pessimistic topics as *Is this the end of the bull market?* or *What should one do today in this kind of a market?* The answer is usually: *Nothing!* In fact, most knowledgeable financial advisors tell their long-term investors to completely ignore the daily market reporting.

I don't doubt that it would be boring if newscasters did nothing but say that the market went up or down so many points in a neutral tone of voice. But surely there is a happy medium. They say the markets are driven by fear and greed. Well, the purveyors of business news at CNBC are doing everything possible to increase the fear part in their thirst for a large and rapt audience.

However understandable in terms of ratings, exaggerating bad news to the public can do a lot of harm. There are no doubt many impressionable people who make ill-advised financial decisions as a direct result of such scare tactics. It would be interesting to know what the effect would be on the market volatility now being experienced if the financial programs spent their time reassuring investors about minor moves in the market instead of fanning hysteria.

There are exceptions, of course. I recall one Friday when a large *plunge* in the market had been reported. The newspaper headline the next day was a one-word quote by that marvelously knowledgeable, solidly reliable Abby Joseph Cohen, who said: *"Relax!"* And, sure enough, that Monday things bounced back nicely. Ms. Cohen often has a reassuring word to say about the markets and would be a better guest to have on programs when things aren't as wildly *on the up-side* as they have been over the last week or two.

FLASH: On January 18, 2011 Steve Jobs of Apple announced without further details that he was taking a medical leave of absence but remaining CEO. In pre-market action, Apple stock fell 5%, losing two weeks worth of gains. While the situation was being discussed by commentators on CNBC, a headline flashed on the screen: "Apple is *sliced*!"

# The Age of Envelope-Pushing

The phrase 'pushing the envelope' appears to have been coined during WWII and refers to the envelope in which the technical specifications and capabilities of an airplane were kept. Pushing the envelope meant pushing the plane beyond its design limits. The phrase has now established itself so firmly in our lexicon and our thinking that our present age could be called the Age of Envelope-Pushing. In every area of our lives we seem to witness a relentless drive to push the envelope in every way. This tendency has been growing for a long time, but never, in my opinion, with the accelerating intensity that we see today.

It is particularly conspicuous in the area of entertainment. In television, even network broadcast TV, producers are constantly flirting with obscene language, total nudity and explicit sex—in other words, outright pornography—to see how far they can go without running afoul of the censors or being taken off the air. Certainly the cable stations have already gone all the way, and anything and everything goes, both visually and verbally. Cable viewers are now treated to depictions of every imaginable sort of sex—heterosexual, homosexual and everything in between, in all shapes and sizes and at every level of indecency and repulsiveness. It has gradually gotten to the point now where it is hard to imagine something in that realm that hasn't already been thoroughly worked over.

Some really classic examples of pushing the envelope can be seen during any of the awards ceremonies coming out of Hollywood, where the real contest is to see how low they can cut the gowns of the young starlets. The idea seems to be to see how much breast area can be exposed without being downright ludicrous or unambiguously sleazy. I sometimes wonder why they don't just go topless, while they're at it. But alas, everyone would quickly get used to that and then more would have to be revealed. Eventually, of course, they couldn't go any further and there would be no more envelope to push. You see, there always has to be some room left to push the envelope or else everyone gets bored. I guess the object is to see how far one can go, how much reaction one can elicit, and still stay barely within, or in the gray zone around, the bounds that are acceptable to contemporary mores.

Meanwhile, cultural mores change all the time; some are progressive, even aggressively progressive, and some are regressive. Certainly the fundamentalists of the various conservative religions have shown us how to be really regressive in cultural mores. The Islamists want to go back several centuries, if not a whole millennium, while the Christians are satisfied to go back merely a century or two.

When it comes to depicting sex on TV and in the movies it would appear that we have nearly exhausted the possibilities as far as envelope-pushing is concerned. After all, what comes after full nudity and fully explicit sex? We are also already pretty far along in the area of violence. Just about everything has been depicted explicitly, except that with violence it is simulated, not real. One can't actually kill or even really maim someone just to make a movie. But much of the sex on the screen is obviously real, and in any case the exhibitionism is real since the people are shown in the nude. Although intercourse is typically only simulated, without actual penetration, still the intimacy of two bodies in even simulated intercourse is experienced as real—and it is pretty close to real, isn't it? What more can be done to push the envelope here, let's say for prime-time broadcast TV? Close-ups of genitalia during actual penetration? Or maybe just close-ups of genitalia themselves? (Of course all of this is already old hat on cable porn channels.) But then what? It's not clear what's left, unless one turns to sadism—real sadism—which of course could be made pretty shocking and would create more opportunities for envelope-pushing.

The so-called reality programs are also already approaching their limits. If the goal is to give people ever new thrills by presenting things that are closer and closer to taboos, there has to come a point beyond which you can't go (that's the taboo). The appeal is in seeing something never seen before, but it has to be something that was once forbidden or inconceivable and is no longer. Maybe we are nearing the point where the entertainment industry will actually have to turn its attention to things that are genuinely interesting and not at all aimed at pushing the envelope or trying to shock, but instead are intended to enlighten and educate through exploration of other aspects of human existence besides sex, violence and greed. The risk, of course, is that this will simply be boring, since the fact remains that most people crave above all stimulation and excitement, whether sexual or otherwise.

On cable TV and in the movies there has for a while now been an unspoken competition to see how many times the F-word can be used in the space of a time slot. This phenomenon is now working its way into network TV. For now it's limited to evening and nighttime broadcasting, but that won't last long, either.

Way back when I was young, in the 1930s, I remember a stage play that was listed by the censors as indecent because the word 'virgin' appeared in the script. (Nowadays, no actor or actress—or anyone over 16, for that matter—would even wish to be thought of as a virgin. Especially for young actresses the very idea undermines the sex-charged image they must try to cultivate.) Years later, viewers were shocked when in *Gone with the Wind* Clark Gable said to Vivian Leigh "I don't give a damn!" Back then, not so terribly long ago, the word damn was infinitely more shocking to audiences than the omnipresent F-word is now.

Nicole Kidman really rammed the envelope full steam ahead recently when she appeared on the Broadway stage 'in the altogether' for a few minutes, thereby attracting a regular contingent of binocular-toting voyeurs to that particular theater. (This phenomenon of fascination with the naked female body probably goes back to the forbidden 'primal scene' in which the child witnesses the parents having sex, and its power is related less to the aesthetics of Ms. Kidman's body than to the fact that this was something never before allowed on Broadway.) However that may be, it definitely pushed Broadway's envelope, even past *The Full Monty*, where nakedness stood more in the service of comedy than forbidden titillation.

Children, of course, have always been interested in seeing how far they can go or how much they can get away with, so to them pushing the envelope comes naturally. But my, how things change! In my day, if you so much as whispered in a class at school you would get 'conduct demerits,' in other words points off for bad behavior, which would actually appear on your report card. Now kids not only whisper in class, they talk right out loud and are not afraid of using the F-word, either. There was a time when you would be sent to the principal's office if you said the word *condom* in class; now they're passing them out in schools! What might be next in the area of adolescent sexuality? Given the way things are going, I can easily imagine that if high school kids started engaging in overt sexual activity—oral sex in the halls, let's say, or in the classroom—the schools might respond by deciding to set aside a private lounge for those who can't control their adolescent urges and where everything would be allowed. That would at least afford some measure of privacy. (A lot of them are doing it at home when mother isn't around anyway, of course. Oral sex is to the teenager of today what necking was to previous generations.) But then again, younger and younger students might insist on having their own lounges, and that would ruin the whole thing for everybody.

But urges are urges, and with the disappearance of controls some sort of accommodation will have to be reached. Teachers tell me that they now do more disciplining than teaching, since kids don't get much discipline at home anymore. Parents, meanwhile, are simply afraid to have confrontations with their kids, so not only does the envelope get pushed, kids can generally assume anything will get by Mom and Pop.

As for the business world, just look at the recent Enron spectacle of personal aggrandizement by a bunch of lying, cheating, greedy high-level creeps in a public corporation at the expense of thousands of everyday people. How flagrant can you get? No wonder members of Congress are scrambling for the exits. Corruption is OK with them within reasonable limits, but the folks at Enron pushed the envelope too far even for our most assiduously envelope-pushing lawmakers.

The automobile industry is making its contribution to envelope-pushing, too. Just look at what's happening with the ubiquitous gas-guzzling, polluting and dangerous SUVs. These are the new status symbols of affluent suburbanites, and it used to be enough that they were enormous, but not anymore. Now they have to be absolutely humongous. There's a new Chevrolet SUV called the Avalanche which in black looks like something that would appeal to Darth Vader. And the new model of the military-styled Hummer is now being enlarged and outfitted with the latest in luxury options to make it the 'just-try-and-outdo-me' vehicle for the keeping-up-with-the-Joneses crowd. It pushes the weight and size envelope for vehicles allowed on passenger-car-only parkways. The next level of envelope-pushing in this area would have to be something like war surplus Sherman tanks tricked out for use by suburban moms. Things really couldn't go beyond that—or could they?

Turning to the business and political world, well, the kind of behavior we see in what used to be respectable circles hardly requires comment. We all know, for instance, about the secret sex lives of past presidents, the high point being the shenanigans of JFK, whose philandering while in the White House was extensive and not very discrete. Even with JFK though, one never heard of explicit sex going on in the Oval Office in broad daylight as we did with Bill Clinton. We have clear evidence that the envelope in this field of endeavor is near the point where it just can't be pushed any further in the fact that Clinton's behavior got him into a lot less trouble that one might have expected. He actually got in more trouble for lying about it than doing it. If I had to try to explain his psychology, I would say it was almost as if he wanted to see how much Hillary would tolerate as a test of her love for him—and he got away with plenty. In the case of JFK, on the other hand, Jackie did apparently take her revenge—or it could be she just felt like having a few flings herself.

Look at the Enron fiasco/scandal. In DC, money talks—*in a really big way*! Everybody and his brother seems to be involved, making it the worst business and political scandal in history. Some people are acting innocent, while others are cutting their losses by giving back some of the really obscene contributions in the hope that they will come up smelling like roses despite everything. Did business people and politicians in the past try to manipulate, lobby and peddle influence to this shocking extent? I think the chiseling and misanthropy, the sheer level of selfishness and greed that we are witnessing today is unprecedented.

What about the music world and the lyrics of contemporary songs? These folks don't just push the envelope—they tear it open and throw it away. Jim Morrison, lead singer and lyricist of the rock band The Doors, started a whole new ball game in his day and enjoyed pushing the envelope as hard as he could, only to self-destruct in the process. He was convicted and sentenced for indecent exposure during a 1969 concert in Miami. During the incident, the police rushed him out of the auditorium as if he had committed an heinous crime. Morrison left the U.S. and moved to Paris, where he died of an apparent drug overdose. His widow claimed recently that his conviction should be posthumously overturned since he did not actually expose himself. Apparently the police were upset by his having simulated masturbation on stage. In his personal life, it turns out, Morrison was battling a disapproving father, but he lost in the end because he was too far ahead of his time in pushing the envelope. We've caught up with him now. The governor of Florida pardoned him in 2010. Just recently an article in the New York Times entitled "Favored Word on the Top 10?" reported that three of the top ten hits on last week's pop music charts included the F-word in their title or lyrics. One was even nominated for a Grammy Award—this despite the fact that the songs had been labeled by the Federal Communications Commission as 'broadcast indecency.'

The Times recently published a photograph of a nude woman, seen from behind, who was one of two framing the visitors' entrance to the Museum of Modern Art. What constitutes indecent exposure nowadays? Would anyone object to two frontally nude women greeting visitors at the entrance to a major museum? Or have times changed?

## The Age of More

The first decade of the 21st century seems to be one of ever more outrageous excesses in all parts of society, so that these days might well one day be called the Age of More. There is more of everything. There are more and bigger show-off trophy houses and more and bigger cars that use up more of everything and kill more people on the roads. There are more excessively wealthy people who seem to want more, and the gulf between them and the working masses is more obvious. There is more blood, violence and explicit sex in our movies, and more still on cable TV. There is more vulgarity—the FCC says we can now hear the F-word used as an adjective, but not as a verb! (Can you believe such nonsense?)

There is more violence in our schools, there are vastly more prisoners in our prison system, and more and more of our mentally ill are inappropriately incarcerated and cruelly treated in our prisons. There is more and more Botox being injected, more and more cosmetic surgery, with even teenage girls getting more and more breast augmentations. We are eating more and there are more obese and morbidly obese people with more and more diabetes, heart disease and other ailments. (Obesity is now the second leading cause of fatal illnesses.) There are more and more signs of depression and anxiety in our population as evidenced by the increasing use of psychotropic medications. There are more and more mothers in the workplace and more and more children being raised by nannies. There is a lot more drug use by high school students and much more precocious sexual activity, too.

In other words, no one seems satisfied with who they are, what they have, what they look like or how big their house or car is. Is there a correlation between these phenomena and the changes that have occurred over the last few generations in our child rearing practices? Children are getting less attention and love from their parents, mothers aren't home as much and families don't eat together as much as they used to. Children, instead of coming home from school to milk and cookies and relaxed play with friends, are now scheduled into more and more highly competitive activities that require lots of car trips and interfere with family meals and evenings.

How to explain these phenomena? Are we more hungry for everything? Is the weakening of religious faith a factor? Is it that parents no longer seem able to inculcate values in their children or even influence their behavior? People are more and more interested in breaking rules and abusing, or at the very least misusing, the freedom our society offers. These questions deserve to be studied, since other societies do not seem inclined to excess in the way that ours does.

## On the Belief in a God

The question *Do you believe in God?* should really be *Do you believe there is a God?*, since the former already implies that there is, in fact, a God and asks merely whether you believe in Him. No one, up to and including the Pope, *knows* that there is a God; it is an article of religious faith. The probability of there being a God is fifty-fifty: there either is or isn't one. Atheists have as much chance of being right as believers.

It has been widely reported that over 90% of Americans say they believe in God. However, the fact that *people say they believe in God* doesn't necessarily mean that they *actually believe that there is a God*. In many places it is quite simply unacceptable, even these days in our society, to say that one does not believe in God, since one is then branded an atheist and made a pariah. Can you imagine any presidential candidate admitting that he or she was an atheist? They might as well hang up the towel from the start. (This may change someday; atheism is the fastest growing 'religious' group in the United States.) This notwithstanding, it seems to me that if one takes a closer look at the behavior of the vast majority of people in this country, one discovers that what they claim to believe does not represent their actual thinking on the subject.

Take, for instance, silent prayer. If silent prayer actually reaches God, it means that all mental activity must somehow make its way to him 24 hours a day, for I doubt that he has some mechanism that only allows prayers to get through. Therefore one must picture human beings as miniature broadcasting stations and all our thoughts, ideas, feelings and wishes are broadcast into space to wherever God exists, where they are continuously monitored. Furthermore, all of this traffic would have to be stored in some gigantic computer-like system in order for the information to be there at the end of one's life so that God could use it to pass judgment and determine the itinerary for one's journey through eternity.

Not only that, but God must constantly receive, 'think' about (if God thinks) and make decisions based on every person's mental activity in order to 'know' whether to answer prayers, evaluate sin, etc. One wonders, for instance, how God decides which prayers to answer and which to ignore (and let's face it—lots are ignored).

In my opinion, if everyone really *knew for certain* that this process was going on, there would be universal panic. Psychiatrists offices would be jammed with people begging for psychotropic medication.

In addition, if everyone *knew for certain* that God was watching what they put in the collection plate, churches wouldn't need to do any more fundraising, church suppers, bake sales and all the other usual activities that bring in pittances. Instead of coins or one-dollar bills in collection plates, there would be fifty-dollar and hundred-dollar bills and fat checks, etc. People would undoubtedly at the very least tithe 10% of their income to their church (as Mormons do). No doubt many generous/fearful souls would make enormous sacrifices and donate large sums to their church in hopes that God would notice and reward them or not punish them for their transgressions, as the case may be. With these vast amounts of money at their disposal, church-based charities could eliminate poverty completely from our society.

If people really *knew for certain* that God was watching and noting their behavior, it would also inevitably have a drastic impact on sexual attitudes and behavior. According to the Bible, *all* sexual activity outside of marriage is fornication. And as St. Paul warned single women and widows regarding fornication, "It is better to marry than to burn." Jesus himself is quoted in several New Testament passages as saying that any divorced person who remarries is committing adultery. According to the Christian Bible therefore, ours is a land of adulterers and fornicators.

People are able to say they *believe in God*, all the while *not really thinking there is a God*, because God has not spoken to or had conversations with anyone in modern times in the way he is reported in the Old Testament to have done long ago. That seems to have stopped after the birth of Christ, aside from the one instance at Jesus' baptism when God is reported to have said, "This is my beloved son in whom I am well pleased." Since then, there has been precious little evidence of that sort in support of God's existence. Nowadays, if someone says they heard or spoke with God, it is assumed that they are either dreaming, hallucinating or lying. No one believes God talks to anyone anymore, except for Pat Robertson.

People are perfectly content to profess belief in God without really believing. Even in the complete absence of tangible evidence it is somehow reassuring to imagine that there is a loving father in heaven looking after us. People like sharing a belief with their fellow human beings and enjoy wishful thinking about a god-like presence somewhere. Human psychology makes it perfectly possible to attest to a belief and at the same time know at a deeper level that it is not true—it happens all the time. Proclaiming one's belief in God is really just a religious person's way of showing that they identify with and subscribe to the values of their community, denomination or congregation. It's also worth noting that there doesn't have to actually be a God in order for belief in God to be emotionally helpful and play an important and positive role in a person's life. Religious faith is also a very potent force for social cohesion, as evidenced by religious communities. But there doesn't actually have to be a God for this to be the case either. There are many different religions worshipping many different Gods, and they all work for their followers.

As a matter of fact, I suspect that most Christians *wouldn't actually want there to be a God*, since if he really did exist and they were convinced of it, they would have to change their behavior drastically in ways they would prefer not to do. Would remarried divorcees and single people who are Christians really want to be under obligation lead celibate lives? Would people really want a situation in which they felt obliged to donate large amounts of money to their church even if it meant significantly sacrificing their standard of living? I think that at some level Christians understandably would see a their God as a nuisance who had the potential to interfere with the pleasures of life and be uncomfortably judgmental. What is curious is that even so, many are reluctant to take a chance and admit to their inner atheism.

In summary, I believe most Americans who say they believe in a God are in denial of the fact that 1) they really don't and 2) they would be mightily put out if He did turn out to exist. The vast majority, of course, don't even want to stop and think about what it all really means; they just say they believe in order to fit in, and let it go at that.

How nice it would be if everyone really did believe in a God. How much less intolerance, hate, dishonesty, violence and other manifestations of human frailty and indifference there would be! Christians, for instance, would actually conduct themselves in accordance with the moral teachings of Christ, and the Christmas spirit would be the order of the day all year long.